Financial Astrology
Almanac
2019

M. G. BUCHOLTZ, B.Sc., MBA

Wood Dragon Books

Box 1216, Regina, Saskatchewan, Canada, S4P 3B4

www.wooddragonbooks.com

ISBN# 978-1-989078-06-8

Financial Astrology Almanac 2019

CONTENTS

Introduction   17

1   Astrology Fundamentals   23

2   The Master Cycle   39

3   Nodes and the 18.6 Year Cycle   41

4   Venus Cycles   45

5   Mercury Cycles   51

6   Professor Weston's Cycles   59

7   Shmitah and Religious Cycles   65

8   Sidereal and Synodic Cycles   73

9   Parallel and Contra Parallel   79

10   New York Stock Exchange 2019 Astrology   89

11   Astrology of Commodities in 2019   129

12   Lines Across Time   203

13   Epilogue   233

14   Glossary of Terms   235

15   Other Books by the Author   239

16   About the Author   243

FIGURES

Figure 1	The Ecliptic	25
Figure 2	The Zodiac Wheel	26
Figure 3	The Planets	27
Figure 4	The Glyphs	28
Figure 5	The Nodes	30
Figure 6	Cardinal Points	32
Figure 7	Synodic and Sidereal Data	34
Figure 8	Superior and Inferior Conjunction	36
Figure 9	Jupiter / Saturn Conjunction in 2000	40
Figure 10	Venus Conjunction and Declination	46
Figure 11	Venus retrograde – The Concept	47
Figure 12	S&P 500 Index and Venus retrograde	48
Figure 13	Venus retrograde and the ASX 200 Index	49
Figure 14	Elongation of Mercury	52
Figure 15	2018 Mercury Elongation events	53
Figure 16	Mercury retrograde – The Concept	54
Figure 17	S&P 500 and Mercury retrograde	55
Figure 18	Mercury retrograde and Copper futures	56
Figure 19	Mercury retrograde and Gold futures	56
Figure 20	Weston's Secondary Cycles	61
Figure 21	Weston's Secondary Maxima	62

Figure 22   Weston's 28 Month Cycle   63

Figure 23   Weston's 20 Month Cycle   64

Figure 24   S&P 500 and Shmitah years   66

Figure 25   Crude Oil and Shmitah years   67

Figure 26   The Aftermath of Shmitah Years   67

Figure 27   Key Hebrew Calendar Dates for 2015   69

Figure 28   Key Hebrew Calendar Dates for 2016   70

Figure 29   Key Hebrew Calendar Dates for 2018   71

Figure 30   Venus Sidereal Cycles   74

Figure 31   Mars Synodic Cycles   75

Figure 32   Moon Declination 2018   76

Figure 33   Moon Geocentric Declination and Soybeans   77

Figure 34   Moon Geocentric Declination and Cotton   78

Figure 35   Gold and Declination Phenomenon   81

Figure 36   Cotton and Declination Phenomenon   83

Figure 37   Crude Oil and Declination Phenomenon   85

Figure 38   Soybeans (1848) and Declination Phenomenon   87

Figure 39   NYSE First Trade horoscope   90

Figure 40   Lunation Event of January, 2016   92

Figure 41   Lunation Event of July, 2017   94

Figure 42   Lunation Event of January, 2018   95

Figure 43   New Moon January 6, 2019   97

Figure 44   New Moon February 4, 2019   98

Figure 45   New Moon March 6, 2019   100

Figure 46   New Moon April 5, 2019   102

Figure 47   New Moon May 4, 2019   104

Figure 48   New Moon June 3, 2019   106

Figure 49   New Moon July 2, 2019   108

Figure 50   New Moon August 1, 2019   1110

Figure 51   New Moon August 30, 2019   112

Figure 52   New Moon September 27, 2019   114

Figure 53   New Moon October 27, 2019   116

Figure 54   New Moon November 26, 2019   118

Figure 55   Houses and Rulers   119

Figure 56   Exaltation and Exile   122

Figure 57   Terms   123

Figure 58   1919 London Gold Fix horoscope   130

Figure 59   Gold futures First Trade horoscope   132

Figure 60   Transiting Mars / natal Sun aspects   133

Figure 61   Transiting Mars / 1919 natal Sun aspects   134

Figure 62   Transiting Sun / 1919 natal Sun aspects   135

Figure 63   Sun conjunct Venus and Gold prices   136

Figure 64   Gold and the Mercury retrograde Influence   137

Figure 65   Silver futures First Trade horoscope   139

Figure 66	Silver futures and Jupiter / natal Sun	140
Figure 67	Silver and Sun/natal Sun events	141
Figure 68	Silver and Mars/natal Sun events	142
Figure 69	Venus Declination and Silver prices	143
Figure 70	Sun Declination and Silver prices	144
Figure 71	Copper futures First Trade horoscope	145
Figure 72	Copper and Mercury retrograde events	146
Figure 73	Pound, Yen, Canadian First Trade horoscope	147
Figure 74	Canadian Dollar Mars conjunct Venus	148
Figure 75	British Pound and Sun passing natal Mars & natal Sun	149
Figure 76	Canadian Dollar and Mercury retrograde	150
Figure 77	Euro Currency First Trade horoscope	151
Figure 78	Sun / Venus Conjunction and the Euro	153
Figure 79	Natal Transits and the Euro Currency	154
Figure 80	First Trade horoscope of Australian Dollar futures	154
Figure 81	First Trade horoscope of Australian Dollar futures	157
Figure 82	Australian Dollar and Mercury Conjunctions	158
Figure 83	Australian Dollar and Sun/natal Sun events	159
Figure 84	First Trade horoscope for 30 Year Bond futures	161
Figure 85	Bonds (30 Year) and Sun in aspect to natal Jupiter	162
Figure 86	30 Year Bonds and Mercury retrograde	163
Figure 87	First Trade horoscope for 10 Year Treasury Notes	165

Figure 88   Mars retrograde and 10 Year Treasuries   166

Figure 89   Mercury retrograde and 10 Year Treasuries   166

Figure 90   First Trade horoscope for Wheat, Corn and Oats futures   167

Figure 91   1848 First Trade horoscope for CBOT   168

Figure 92   Corn prices and Sun/natal Sun events   169

Figure 93   Corn prices and Mars/natal Sun events   170

Figure 94   Corn prices and Mars Declination   171

Figure 95   Wheat prices and Venus Declination   172

Figure 96   Wheat prices and Mercury retrograde events   173

Figure 97   Soybeans First Trade horoscope   174

Figure 98   Soybeans and Sun/natal Sun events   175

Figure 99   Soybeans and Mars/natal Sun events   176

Figure 100   Soybeans and Mercury events   178

Figure 101   Soybeans and Venus Declination   179

Figure 102   Crude Oil First Trade horoscope   181

Figure 103   Crude Oil and Mars transits   182

Figure 104   Crude Oil and Sun transits   183

Figure 105   Crude Oil and Mercury retrograde events   184

Figure 106   Crude Oil and Venus retrograde events   185

Figure 107   Cotton futures First Trade horoscope   187

Figure 108   Cotton futures and Sun/natal Sun aspects   188

Figure 109   Cotton futures and Venus/natal Moon aspects   189

Figure 110   Coffee futures First Trade horoscope   191

Figure 111   Coffee prices and natal transits   192

Figure 112   Coffee prices and Sun/Uranus aspects   193

Figure 113   Sugar Futures First Trade horoscope   195

Figure 114   Sugar prices and natal transits   196

Figure 115   Mercury retrograde and Sugar price   197

Figure 116   Cocoa futures First Trade horoscope   199

Figure 117   Mercury retrograde and Cocoa price   200

Figure 118   Cocoa price and Mercury cycles   201

Figure 119   Gann Lines applied to a Gold Chart   205

Figure 120   Gann Lines and Gold 2018   206

Figure 121   Gann Lines and Gold 2019   206

Figure 122   Gann Lines applied to a Crude Oil chart   208

Figure 123   Updated Gann Lines and Crude Oil
                                                            209

Figure 124   Crude Oil and Uranus Transit Lines   210

Figure 125   Crude Oil and Uranus Transit Lines 2018   210

Figure 126   Dow Jones Average and Mars Transit Lines   211

Figure 127   Dow Jones and Mars Transit Lines 2018   212

Figure 128   ASX 200 and Jupiter Transit Lines 2018   212

ACKNOWLEDGMENTS

To the many traders and investors who at some visceral level suspect there is more to the financial market complex than P/E ratios and analyst recommendations. You are correct. There is more. Much more. The markets are rooted in astronomical and astrological timing. This book will add a whole new dimension to your market activities.

DISCLAIMER

All material provided herein is based on material gleaned from mathematical and astrological publications researched by the author to supplement his own trading. This publication is written with sincere intent for those who actively trade and invest in the financial markets and who are looking to incorporate astrological phenomena and esoteric math into their market activity. While the material presented herein has proven reliable to the author in his personal trading and investing activity, there is no guarantee the material herein will continue to be reliable into the future. The author and publisher assume no liability whatsoever for any investment or trading decisions made by readers of this book. The reader alone is responsible for all trading and investment outcomes and is further advised not to exceed his or her risk tolerances when trading or investing on the financial markets.

Recommended Readings

Astrology Really Works, edited by Jill Kramer for The Magi Society, (Hay House Inc, USA, 1995)

The Bull, the Bear and the Planets, M.G. Bucholtz, (iUniverse, USA, 2013)

The Lost Science, M.G. Bucholtz, (iUniverse, USA, 2013)

Stock Market Forecasting – The McWhirter Method De-Mystified, M.G. Bucholtz, (Wood Dragon Books, Canada, 2014)

The Cosmic Clock, M.G. Bucholtz (Wood Dragon Books, Canada, 2016)

The Universal Clock, J. Long, (P.A.S. Publishing, USA,)

McWhirter Theory of Stock Market Forecasting, L. McWhirter, (Astro Book Company, USA, 1938)

The Universe Within, N. Turok, (House of Anansi Press, Canada, 2012)

A Theory of Continuous Planet Interaction, Tony Waterfall, NCGR Research Journal, Volume 4, Spring 2014, pp 67-87.

Financial Astrology, Giacomo Albano, (Amazon, U.K., 2011)

Introduction

Many market analysts and financial media commentators think daily news, quarterly earnings reports and corporate events drive stock prices.

I disagree.

There is something else that drives the financial markets. I have two opinions on what this something else might be.

The first opinion is that the financial markets are a reflection of the mass psychological emotion of traders, investors and fund managers. The term *reflection* may even be too mild of a descriptor. It may be more accurate to boldly state that human emotion drives buying and selling decisions in the financial markets. When market participants are feeling positive, they are driven to buy. When they are feeling uncertain or negative, they are driven to sell.

Probing this idea deeper immediately yields the complex question - what drives human emotion?

Medical researchers still have not definitively answered this question. Some say changes in blood alkalinity or acidity impact our emotions. Some say changes in chemical hormones in the bloodstream are the cause. My humble opinion on this complex matter is that the ever-changing configurations of orbiting planets and other celestial bodies in our cosmos influence our body chemistry and thereby drive human emotion.

This opinion has been shaped by the many Astrology publications I have read over the past several years including Tony Waterfall's insightful article from the Spring 2014 NCGR Research Journal. In his article Waterfall reminds readers that the Sun is the centre of our planetary system. The Sun emits massive amounts of solar radiation in all directions into the vastness of space. This radiation is called *solar wind*. This solar wind interacts with the magnetic fields around Mercury,

Venus, Moon, Mars, Jupiter, Saturn, Uranus, Neptune and Pluto. These planets accept and then disburse the solar wind radiation. As the radiation is disbursed, a goodly amount of it finds its way towards the magnetic field around planet Earth. Changes in the density and speed of solar wind mean that the amount of radiation reaching Earth's magnetic field on a daily, weekly or monthly basis will be ever-changing. As a result, the intensity or flux of the Earth's magnetic field is also constantly changing. The alignment of the orbiting planets at any given time in our cosmos plays a key role in determining how much solar radiation is deflected towards Earth's magnetic field. A simplistic way of viewing this entire arrangement is to think of a billiards table as the cosmos. The various balls on the table are the planets and other celestial bodies. The solar radiation is the white cue ball bouncing and deflecting off other balls on the table. Add to this line of reasoning the fact that the human body is largely comprised of water. We all have an electrical field that runs through our tissues. Hence, basic physics demands that changes to the Earth's magnetic field will then induce subtle changes to our bodily electric circuitry. These subtle changes, in my opinion, are what drive our emotional responses. But there is so much more to be understood. Scientists and psychologists who are on a quest to learn more have come to call the developing science of how the cosmos affects humans, *cosmo-biology*.

Ancient civilizations as far back as the Babylonians too recognized cosmo-biology, but in a more rudimentary form. Their high priests tracked and recorded changes in the emotions of the people. These diviners and seers also tracked events, both fortuitous and disastrous. Although they lacked the ability to comprehend the physics of solar wind and magnetic fields, they were able to visually spot planets Mercury, Venus, Mars, Jupiter and Saturn in the heavens. They correlated changes in human emotion and changes in societal events to these planets. They assigned to these planets the names of the various Deities revered by the people. They further identified and named various star constellations in the heavens and further divided the heavens into twelve signs. This was the birth of Astrology as we know it today.

My second opinion on what drives financial markets is a brazen one. This opinion bluntly says that the markets are manipulated from deep within New York, London and other financial centers. This manipulation is based around astrological cycles and occurrences. It is then quite possible that once efforts to "move" the markets are underway at these various points in time, human emotion kicks in and media frenzy takes over.

Starting in the early 1900's, esoteric thinkers such as the famous Wall Street trader W.D. Gann noted that basic Astrology bore a striking correlation to changes on the financial markets. This was the birth of Financial Astrology. Gann based his writings and forecasts on the synodic cycles between various planets. Gann also delved deep into esoteric math, notably square root math. He is well remembered for Gann Lines – a technique based on square roots. But Gann lived in a challenging time. Statute laws in places like New York expressly forbade the use of occult science in business ventures. Gann therefore carefully concealed the basis for his market forecasts. Today many traders and investors try to emulate Gann but they do so in a linear fashion – looking for repetitive cycles on the calendar. What they are missing is the Astrology component, which is anything but linear.

In the 1930s, Louise McWhirter followed closely in Gann's footsteps. She identified an 18.6 year cyclical correlation between the general state of the American economy and the position of the North Node of Moon. Her methodology also extended to include the transiting Moon passing by key points of the 1792 natal birth horoscope of the New York Stock Exchange. As well, she identified a correlation between price movement of a stock and those times when transiting Sun, Mars, Jupiter and Saturn made hard aspects to the natal Sun position in the stock's natal birth (first trade) horoscope.

The late 1940s saw even further advancements in the field of Financial Astrology when astrologer Garth Allen (a.k.a. Donald Bradley) produced his Siderograph Model. This complex model is based on aspects between the various transiting planets. Each aspect as it occurs is given a sinusoidal weighting as the *orb* (separation) between the planets varies. This model is as powerful today as it was in the late 1940s.

As you read these words, I invite you to think back to the dark days of late 2008 when there was genuine concern over the very survival of the financial market system. This timeframe was the end of an 18.6 year cycle of the North Node traveling around the zodiac. To those players at high levels in the financial system who understand Astrology, this period was a prime opportunity to feast off the fear of the investing public and off the fear of government officials who were standing at the ready with lucrative bailout packages. Think more recently to August 2015 and the market selloff that apparently nobody saw coming. The reality is that this selloff started at a confluence of two events. August 2015 marked a Venus retrograde event and the appearance of Venus as a morning star after having been only visible as an evening star for the past 263 days. What about the early days of 2016 when Mercury was retrograde and the markets hit a rough patch? What about the weakness of June 2016 when Venus emerged from conjunction to become visible as an Evening Star? And how about the dire predictions for financial market calamity following the election of Donald Trump to the White House? When the markets instead powered higher, analysts were flummoxed. It turns out, Venus was making its declination minima right at the time of the US election. Such declination minima bear a striking correlation to changes of trend on US equity markets. What about the early days of 2018 when again fear gripped the system? This was Venus at its declination low. Markets reached a turning point in the first week of October 2018 which again was Venus at a declination low. Add the fact that Venus turned retrograde at the same time and the fear all starts to make sense.

I personally began to embrace Financial Astrology in 2012 which was a monumental shift given that my educational background comprises an Engineering degree and an MBA degree. As I pen the text for this 2019 Almanac, I find myself again at school, this time in pursuit of a M.Sc. degree. Three linear-thinking, left-brain degrees to be sure. Since 2012, my research and back-testing has satisfied me that a correlation does indeed exist between Astrology and the financial markets. This Almanac represents my tenth publication on the subject of Financial Astrology.

This Almanac begins by offering you a fairly thorough look at the cyclical math and science of Astrology. What then follows is an examination of the New York Stock Exchange for the twelve months of calendar year 2019. Each monthly examination presents a summation of key dates when Astrology events make a high probability of influencing human emotion. A look at various commodity futures and the astro phenomena that influence them then follows. Also in this Almanac, I provide a look at Gann Lines and Quantum Price Lines, two esoteric mathematical concepts that should be used when applying Astrology to make trading and investing decisions. I further offer some valuable market insights based on planetary declinations and planetary cycles. I even go so far as to examine religious celebratory dates including the concept of *Shmitah* as alternative ways of measuring time.

When applying Astrology to trading and investing, it is vital at all times to be aware of the price trend. There are many ways of observing trend. My personal experience has shown me that the chart indicators developed by J. Welles Wilder are very effective at identifying trend changes. In particular, the DMI and the Volatility Stop are two indicators that should be taken seriously. As a trader and investor, what you are looking for is a change of trend that aligns to an Astrology event. When you see the trend change, you should take action. Whether that action is implementing a long position, a short position, an Options strategy or just tightening up on a stop loss will depend on your personal appetite for risk and on your investment and trading objectives. Astrology is not about trying to take action at each and every astro event that comes along because not all astro events are powerful enough to induce a change of trend. This Almanac is designed to be a resource for you to help you stay abreast of the various astro events that 2019 holds in store.

I sincerely hope after you have applied the material in this Almanac to your trading and investing activity, you will embrace Financial Astrology as a valuable tool.

To further set the tone for what you are about to read in this Almanac, I leave you with the following quotes on the subject of Astrology:

"An unfailing experience of mundane events in harmony with the changes occurring in the heavens, has instructed and compelled my unwilling belief."
(Johannes   Kepler,   astronomer   and   mathematician   1571-1630)

"Heaven sends down its good and evil symbols and wise men act accordingly."
(Confucius – Chinese philosopher 551-479 BC)

"The controls of life are structured as forms and nuclear arrangements, in relation with the motions of the universe." (Louis Pasteur-scientist 1822-1895)

"Oh the wonderful knowledge to be found in the stars. Even the smallest things are written   there…if   you   had   but   skill   to   read."
(Ben Franklin-one of the Founding Fathers of America 1706-1790)

"It's common knowledge that a large percentage of Wall Street brokers use Astrology." (Donald Reagan, formerly Ronald Reagan's Chief of Staff)

1

Astrology Fundamentals

Astrology is an ancient science focused on the correlation between the planets, events of nature and behaviour of mankind. This ancient science is rooted in thousands of years of observation across many civilizations.

- The ancient Sumerians, Akkadians and Babylonians between the 4th and 2nd centuries BC believed the affairs of mankind could be gauged by watching the motions of certain stars and planets. They recorded their predictions and future indications of prosperity and calamity on clay tablets. These early recordings form the foundation of modern day Astrology.

- Ancient Egyptian artifacts show that high priests Petosiris and Necepso who lived during the reign of Ramses II were revered for their knowledge of Astrology. The Egyptian culture is thought to have developed a 12 month x 30 day time keeping method based on the repeated appearances of constellations.

- Ancient Indian and Chinese artifacts reveal that Astrology held an esteemed place in those societies for many thousands of years.

- Hipparchus, Pythagoras and Plato are key names from the Greek era. Historians think Pythagoras assigned mathematical values to the relations between celestial bodies. Plato is thought to have offered up predictions relating celestial bodies to human fates. Hipparchus is thought to have compiled a star catalogue which popularized Astrology.

- In the latter years of the Roman empire, Astrology was used for political gain. Important military figures surrounded themselves with philosophers such as Ptolemy and Valens. In 126 AD, Ptolemy penned four books describing the influence of the stars. His works are collectively called the *Tetrabiblos*. In 160

AD, Valens penned *Anthologies* in which he further summarized the principles of Astrology.

Following the conversion of Emperor Constantine to Christianity in 312 AD, using Astrology for gain became a crime according to the Church of Rome. Astrology then began a slow retreat to the sidelines where for the most part it remains today. Despite having been sidelined by a Church seeking to protect its authority, Astrology quietly continued in use by leading thinkers of the day such as Galileo, Brahe, Nostradamus, Kepler, Bacon and Newton. Thanks to the tenacity of these men, Astrology was prevented from fading away altogether into a distant memory.

The Ecliptic and the Zodiac

The Sun is at the center of our solar system. The Earth, Moon, planets and various other asteroid bodies complete our planetary system. The various planets and other asteroid bodies rotate 360 degrees around the Sun following a path called the *ecliptic plane* as shown in Figure 1. Earth (and its Equator) is slightly tilted (approximately 23.5 degrees) relative to the ecliptic plane. Projecting the Earth's equator into space produces the *celestial equator plane*. There are two points of intersection between the ecliptic plane and celestial equator plane. These points are commonly called the *vernal equinox* (occurring at March 20th) and the *autumnal equinox* (occurring at September 20th). You will otherwise recognize these dates as the first day of Spring and the first day of Fall, respectively. Dividing the ecliptic plane into twelve equal sections of 30 degrees results in what astrologers call the *zodiac*. The twelve portions of the zodiac have names including Aries, Cancer, Leo and so on. Ancient civilizations looking skyward identified patterns of stars called constellations that align to these twelve zodiac divisions. If these names sound familiar, they should. You routinely see all twelve names in the daily horoscope section of your morning newspaper.

The Glyphs

Figure 2 illustrates a *zodiac wheel*. In Figure 2, you will notice that these twelve divisions of the ecliptic have each been assigned a peculiar looking symbol. These symbols are called *glyphs*.

The starting point or zero degree point of the zodiac wheel is the sign Aries, located at the *vernal equinox* of each year. The vernal equinox is what we regard as the start of Spring each year. The *autumnal equinox* is what we regard as the start of Autumn each year.

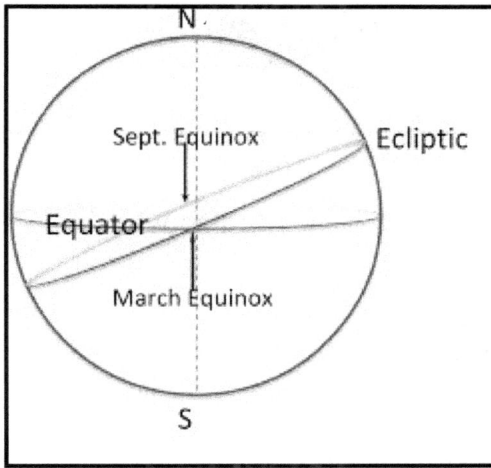

Figure 1 The Ecliptic

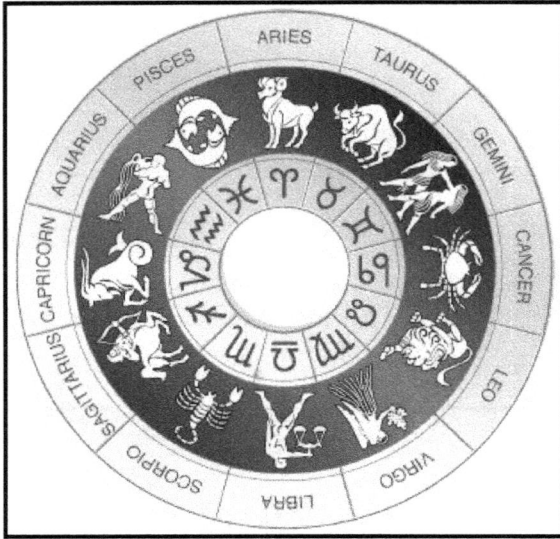

Figure 2 The Zodiac Wheel

The Celestial Bodies

In addition to the Sun and Moon, there are eight celestial bodies important to the application of Astrology to trading and investing on the financial markets. These planets are Mercury, Venus, Mars, Jupiter, Saturn, Uranus, Neptune and Pluto. Figure 3 illustrates these various bodies in orbit around the Sun on the ecliptic plane.

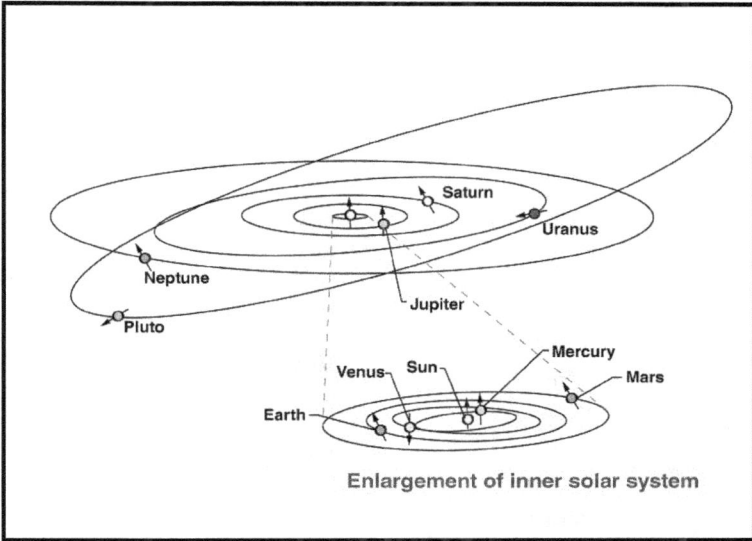

Enlargement of inner solar system

Figure 3 The Planets

These planets are also denoted by *glyphs*. Figure 4 presents these glyphs along with the zodiac sign glyphs.

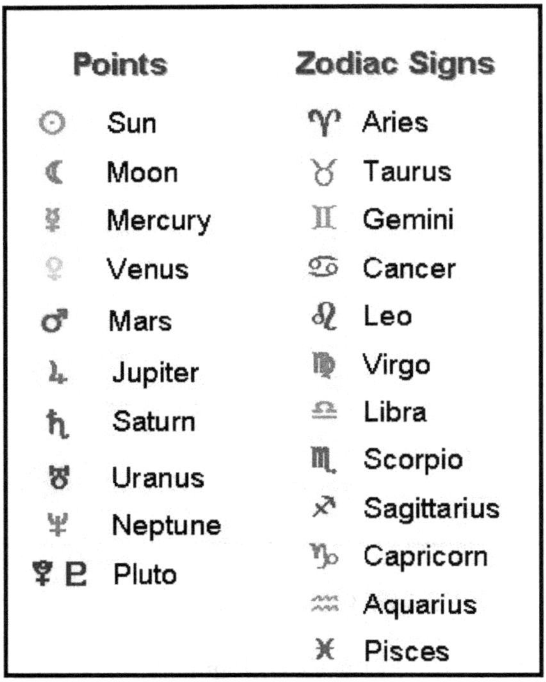

Points		Zodiac Signs	
☉	Sun	♈	Aries
☽	Moon	♉	Taurus
☿	Mercury	♊	Gemini
♀	Venus	♋	Cancer
♂	Mars	♌	Leo
♃	Jupiter	♍	Virgo
♄	Saturn	♎	Libra
♅	Uranus	♏	Scorpio
♆	Neptune	♐	Sagittarius
♇ ♇	Pluto	♑	Capricorn
		♒	Aquarius
		♓	Pisces

Figure 4 The Glyphs

Declination

As the various celestial bodies make their respective journeys around the Sun, they can be seen to move relative to our vantage point of the celestial equator. Declination refers to this positioning of a celestial body above or below the celestial equator plane. Celestial bodies experience declinations of up to about 25 degrees above and below the celestial equator plane.

Mercury, Venus and Mars endure frequent changes in declination due to the gravitational force of the Sun. Planets like Jupiter, Saturn, Neptune, Uranus and Pluto also experience declination changes but these changes are slow to evolve. As this book will illustrate, changes in the declination of a celestial body can affect the financial markets. In particular, Venus and Mars have a notable effect.

Parallel and Contra-Parallel

Declination can be viewed one planet at a time or by pairs of planets. Let's suppose that at a particular time Mars can be seen as being 10 degrees of declination above the celestial equator and at that same time Venus is also at 10 degrees of declination. Let's further suppose that we allow for up to 1.5 degrees tolerance in our measurement of declinations. We would say these two planets were at *parallel declination*. Let's take another example and suppose that at a given time Jupiter was at 5 degrees of declination above the celestial equator and at that same time period Pluto was at 6 degrees declination below the celestial equator. Again, let's allow for up to 1.5 degrees of tolerance. We would say that Jupiter and Pluto were at *contra-parallel declination*. As this Almanac will show, parallel and contra-parallel events have a powerful bearing on certain aspects of the financial markets.

The Moon

Just as the planets orbit 360 degrees around the Sun, the Moon orbits 360 degrees around the Earth. The Moon orbits the Earth in a plane of motion called the *lunar orbit plane*. This plane is inclined at about 5 degrees to the ecliptic plane as Figure 5 shows. The Moon orbits Earth with a slightly elliptical pattern in approximately 27.3 days, relative to an observer located on a fixed frame of reference such as the Sun. This time period is known as a *sidereal month*. However, during one sidereal month, an observer located on Earth (a moving frame of reference) will revolve part way around the Sun. To that Earth-bound observer, a complete orbit of the Moon around the Earth will appear longer than the sidereal month at approximately 29.5 days. This 29.5 day period of time is known as a *synodic month* or more commonly a *lunar month*. The lunar month plays a key role in applying Astrology to the financial markets as will be detailed throughout this book.

The Moon figures prominently in the history and lore of Astrology. Throughout the centuries, the Moon has been associated with health, mood and dreams. In 6th century Constantinople (modern day

Istanbul, Turkey), physicians at the court of Emperor Justinian advised that gout could be cured by inscribing verses of Homer on a copper plate when the Moon was in the sign of Libra or Leo. In 17th century France, astrologers used the Moon to explain mood changes in women. In 17th century England, herbal remedy practitioners advised people to pluck the petals of the peony flower when the Moon was waning. During the Renaissance period, it was thought that dreams could come true if the Moon was in the signs of Taurus, Leo, Aquarius or Scorpio.

Today, such ideas about the Moon are no more. But, the Moon nonetheless continues to be recognized as a powerful celestial body. Just as the gravitational pull of the Moon can influence the action of ocean tides, this same pull somehow also influences our emotions of fear and hope. As our emotions of fear and hope change, our investment buying and selling decisions also change. These emotional changes correlate to changes in price trend action. When this correlation is overlaid with technical chart analysis, a whole new dimension in trading and investing opens up as this book will detail.

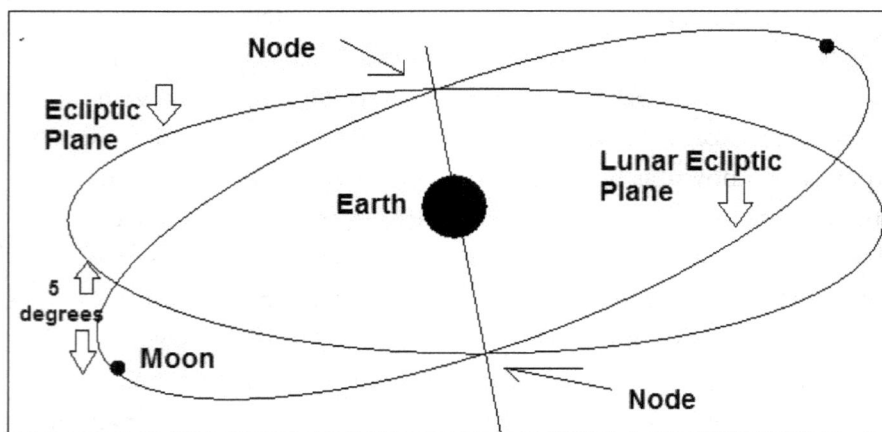

Figure 5 The Nodes

The Nodes

Another mathematical construct central to Financial Astrology is the Nodes. The Nodes are the points of intersection between the ecliptic plane and the Moon's ecliptic plane. Figure 5 also illustrates the Nodes. In Astrology, typically only the North Node is referred to. The importance of the North Node will be emphasized later in this Almanac when the McWhirter Method is discussed.

Eclipses

A Solar eclipse occurs when the Moon passes through a Node during a New Moon event. A Lunar eclipse occurs when the Moon passes through a Node during a Full Moon event.

As observed from the Earth, a solar eclipse occurs when the Moon passes in front of the Sun. The type of solar eclipse event depends on the distance of the Moon from the Earth during the event. A total solar eclipse occurs when the Earth is completely blanketed by Moon's shadow. Annular and partial eclipses occur when the Earth is only partially blanketed by the Moon's shadow.

Lunar eclipses occur when the Moon is on the far side of the Earth from the Sun. Lunar eclipses only occur at a Full Moon event.

Ascendant, Descendant, MC and IC

As the Earth rotates on its axis once in every 24 hours, an observer situated on Earth will detect an apparent motion of the constellation stars that define the zodiac. To better define this motion, astrologers apply four cardinal points to the zodiac, almost like the north, south, east and west points on a compass. These cardinal points divide the zodiac into four quadrants. The east point is termed the *Ascendant* and is often abbreviated Asc. The west point is termed the *Descendant* and is often abbreviated Dsc. The south point is termed the *Mid-Heaven* (from the Latin *Medium Coeli*) and is often abbreviated MC or MH. The north point is termed the *Imum Coeli* (Latin for bottom of the sky) and is abbreviated IC. Figure 6 illustrates the placement of these cardinal points on a typical zodiac wheel. The importance of the Ascendant and Mid-Heaven will be emphasized later in this Almanac when the McWhirter Method is discussed.

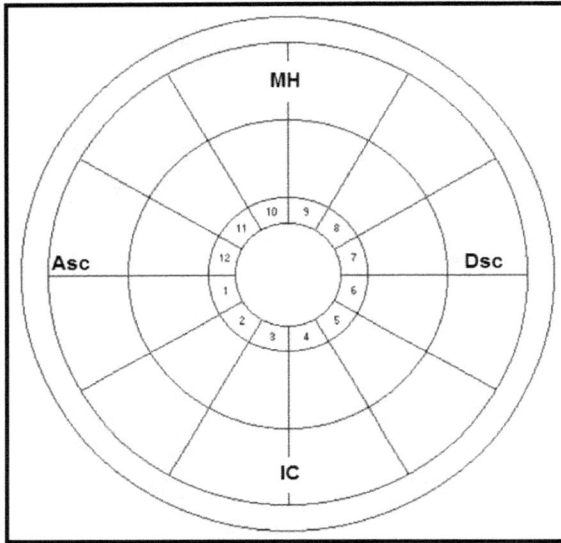

Figure 6 Cardinal Points

Geocentric and Heliocentric Astrology

Astrology comes in two distinct varieties – *geocentric* and *heliocentric*.

In *geocentric* Astrology, the Earth is the vantage point for observing the planets as they pass through the signs of the zodiac. Owing to the different times for the planets to each orbit the Sun, an astrologer situated on Earth would see the planets making distinct angles (called *aspects*) with one another and also with the Sun. The aspects that are commonly used in Astrology are 0, 30, 45, 60, 90, 120, 150 and 180 degrees. In Financial Astrology, it is common to refer to only the 0, 90, 120 and 180 degree aspects.

In *heliocentric* Astrology, the Sun is the vantage point for observing the planets as they pass through the signs of the zodiac. An observer positioned on the Sun would also see the orbiting planets making aspects with one another.

To identify these aspects, astrologers use Ephemeris Tables. For geocentric Astrology, the *New American Ephemeris for the 21ˢᵗ Century* is commonly used. It is available at most bookstores. For heliocentric Astrology, the *American Heliocentric Ephemeris* is a good resource. It tends to be harder to find in bookstores but on-line booksellers should have it available.

For faster aspect determination, two excellent software programs available are *Millenium Trax* produced by AIR Software and *Solar Fire Gold* produced by Astrolabe. My preference is the *Solar Fire Gold* product. I also use a market platform called Market Analyst. This brilliant piece of software, (originally developed in Australia) allows the user to generate an end of day price chart for equities and commodities from a multitude of exchanges and then overlay various astrological aspects and occurrences onto the chart. In my not so humble opinion, all serious adherents of Financial Astrology should spend the money to acquire this software program.

To investigate Market Analyst Software, follow this link to take it for a free test-drive.

www.mav8.com/investingsuccess

Synodic and Sidereal

The vantage point of either Earth or Sun then leads to two more concepts – synodic and sidereal. To an earth-bound observer, a synodic time period is the time between two successive occurrences. That is, how many days does it take for Sun passing Pluto on the zodiac wheel to again pass Pluto? To a Sun-bound observer, a sidereal time period is the number of days (or years) it takes for a planet to orbit the Sun. These time frames play roles in assessing market cycles as will be discussed in this Almanac. Figure 7 presents synodic and sidereal data.

Planet	Synodic Period	Sidereal Period
Mercury	116 days	88 days
Venus	584 days	225 days
Mars	780 days	1.9 years
Jupiter	399 days	11.9 years
Saturn	378 days	29.5 years
Uranus	370 days	84 years
Neptune	368 days	164.8 years
Pluto	367 days	248.5 years

Figure 7 Synodic and Sidereal Data

Retrograde

Think of the planets orbiting the Sun as a group of race cars travelling around a racetrack. Consider what happens as a fast moving car approaches a slower moving car from behind. At first, all appears normal. An observer in the fast moving car sees the slower moving car heading in the same direction. Gradually, the observer in the fast car sees that he will soon overtake the slow car. For a brief moment in time as the fast car overtakes the slower car the observer in the fast car notices that the slower car appears to stand still and even move backwards. Of course the slow car is not really standing still. This is simply an optical illusion.

These brief illusory periods are what astrologers call retrograde events. To ancient societies, retrograde events were of great significance as human emotion was often seen to be changeable at these events.

From the vantage point of an observer on Earth, there will be three or four times during a year when Earth and Mercury pass by each other on this celestial racetrack. There will be one or perhaps two times per year when Earth and Venus pass each other. There will be one time every two years when Earth and Mars pass each other.

Elongation and Separation

The orbit of a planet around the Sun is not a perfectly circular event. Rather, planets orbit the Sun in elliptical paths. For example, Mercury orbits the Sun in about 88 days. There will be times in its elliptical orbit when it is far from the Sun and there will be times when it is close to the Sun. More specifically, the times when a planet is farthest from the Sun are called Perihelion events or Perigee events. Times when a planet is closest to the Sun are called Aphelion events or Apogee events.

This phenomenon applies to the Moon in its path around the Earth as well. Apogee events occur when the Moon is closest to Earth. Perigee events occur when Moon is farthest from Earth.

From an observers vantage point on Earth, there will also be times when planets are seen to be at maximum angles of separation from the Sun. These events are what astronomers refer to as maximum easterly and westerly elongations.

Conjunctions

Mercury and Venus are closer to the Sun than is the Earth. From our vantage point on Earth, there will be times when Mercury or Venus are between us and the Sun. Likewise, there will be times when the Sun is between us and Mercury or Venus. On the zodiac wheel, the times when Mercury or Venus are at the same zodiac sign and degree as the Earth are what astronomers call conjunctions.

An *Inferior Conjunction* occurs with Mercury or Venus between Earth and the Sun. A *Superior Conjunction* occurs with the Sun between Earth and Mercury or Venus. Figure 8 illustrates further.

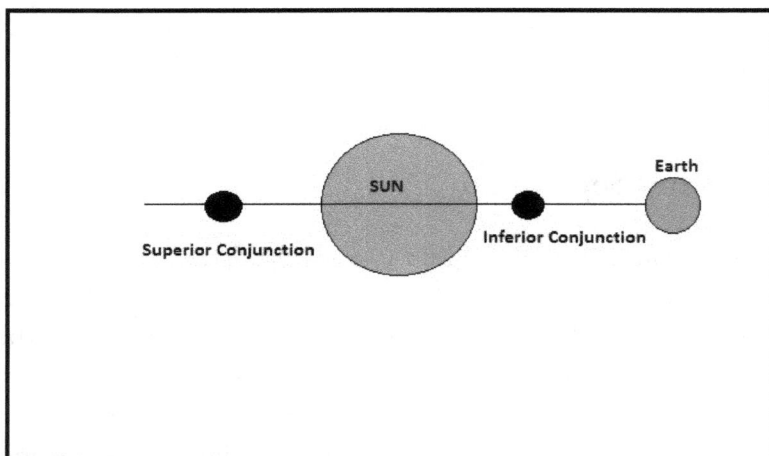

Figure 8 Superior and Inferior Conjunction

Conjunction events are closely related to retrograde events in that they occur on either side of retrograde events. For example, in 2018 Venus was retrograde from October 5 to November 15. Its actual Inferior Conjunction was recorded on October 26.

After Venus has been at Inferior Conjunction, it will be visible as a Morning Star. After it has been at Superior Conjunction it will be visible as an Evening Star. Venus was at Superior Conjunction on March 28, 2013 (8 Aries), October 25, 2014 (1 Scorpio), June 6, 2016 (16 Gemini) and January 8, 2018 (18 Capricorn). Venus was at Inferior Conjunction on June 6, 2012 (15 Gemini), January 11, 2014 (21 Capricorn), August 15, 2015 (22 Leo), March 25, 2017 (4 Aries), and October 26, 2018 (3 Scorpio). Plot these groups of Superior Conjunction events on a zodiac wheel. Note how they can be joined to form a 5-pointed star called a pentagram. Likewise, the Inferior Conjunction events can be plotted and joined to form a pentagram. Such is the elegance and mystique of the cosmos.

2

The Master Cycle

Having touched on the basics of Astrology in the previous chapter, let's start a closer examination of Financial Astrology with a look at a long cycle that the venerable W.D. Gann called the Master Cycle.

Gann closely followed the orbital periods of Jupiter and Saturn. To an observer situated on a fixed vantage point such as the Sun, Jupiter would be seen orbiting the Sun in about 12 years and Saturn in just over 29 years. But, Gann took his observations one step further and noted that every 20 or so years, Jupiter and Saturn were at conjunction, separated by zero degrees. Gann further noted that the financial markets seemed to be affected by these conjunction events of Jupiter and Saturn. The market crash of 1901 aligned to a conjunction of these two outer planets. In 1920, the U.S. economy encountered a recession and in 1921 the financial markets reached a low point, again at the conjunction of these two heavy-weight planets. In 1941, the markets recorded a low point a couple months after another Jupiter-Saturn conjunction. In early 1960s, the Jupiter-Saturn conjunction aligned to a drawdown in the U.S. equity markets that historians now call the Kennedy Slide. However, following this event, markets recovered and actually made new highs into the 4th quarter of 1965 when a major turning point was encountered. This turning point was a Cardinal Cross. Picture a rectangle with parallel sides and parallel ends. The corner points of the rectangle are pairs of planets. This most unique and powerful formation involving eight planets (Neptune was the odd man out) gave rise to a significant turning point on the market. It would not be until 1995 when the market would again test this level.

In more recent memory, in the Spring of 1981, Jupiter and Saturn recorded a conjunct event. A handful of months later, the U.S. equity markets recorded a very important low that marked the onset of a massive bull market that ran until the next conjunction event in mid-2000. If you were around then, the mention of the tech-bubble probably brings back painful memories of money lost in your brokerage account. Figure 9 illustrates how the S&P 500 was making its peak as Jupiter and Saturn were making their conjunction.

Figure 9 Jupiter / Saturn Conjunction in 2000

We are now within eyesight of the next conjunction event which will arrive in the middle of 2020, leading up to the U.S. Presidential election. This conjunction event could be a powerful one as the zodiac chart shows 8 planets crammed into a 90 degree segment of the chart. That is a lot of concentrated planetary energy. The time to start strategizing for this event is right now if you wish to avoid a repeat savage repeat brutalizing of your investment account.

3

North Node and the 18.6 Year Cycle

There exists another longer cycle that people ought to be more aware of. This cycle was first written about in the 1930s by a mysterious figure called Louise McWhirter. I say mysterious because in all my travels I have not come across any other writings by her nor have I found much reference to her in other manuscripts. I am almost of the opinion that the name might have been a pseudonym for someone seeking to disseminate astrological ideas while remaining anonymous.

McWhirter recognized that the transit of the North Node around the zodiac wheel takes 18.6 years and that the Node progresses in a backwards motion through the zodiac signs. Recall from the Astrology Fundamentals chapter that the Moon orbits the Earth in a plane of motion called the Lunar Ecliptic. Two planes that are not parallel will always intersect at two points. The two points where the Lunar Ecliptic intersects that plane of motion of planet Earth are termed the North Node and South Node. Through examination of copious amounts of economic data provided by Leonard P. Ayers of the Cleveland Trust Company, she was able to conclude that when the North Node moves through certain zodiac signs, the economic business cycle reaches a low point and when the Node is in certain other signs, the business cycle is at its strongest. This line of thinking is still with us today. As an aside - in your travels try to find writings by economist Fred Harrison. He discusses these long economic cycles but, to maintain respect in academic circles, he stops just shy of stating a connection to Astrology.

In particular, McWhirter was able to discern the following:

• As the Node enters Aquarius, the low point of economic activity has been reached

- As the Node leaves Aquarius and begins to transit through Capricorn and Sagittarius, the economy starts to return to normal

- As the Node passes through Scorpio and Libra, the economy is functioning above normal

- As the Node transits through Leo, the high point in economic activity has been reached

- As the Node transits through Cancer and Gemini, the economy is easing back towards normal

- As the Node enters the sign of Taurus, the economy begins to slow

- As the Node enters Aquarius, the low point of economic activity has been reached and a full 18.6 year cycle has been completed.

McWhirter further observed some secondary factors that could influence the tenor of economic activity in a good way, no matter which sign the Node was in at the time:

- Jupiter being 0 degrees conjunct to the Node

- Jupiter being in Gemini or Cancer

- Pluto being at a favorable aspect to the Node

McWhirter also observed some secondary factors that can influence the tenor of economic activity in a bad way, no matter which sign the Node was in at the time:

- Saturn being 0, 90 or 180 degrees to the Node

- Saturn in Gemini or Cancer

- Uranus in Gemini

- Uranus being 0, 90 or 180 degrees to the Node

- Pluto being at an unfavorable aspect to the Node

So, where are we now? What does 2019 portend? You have no doubt heard the media making rumblings about a looming recession. The zodiac shows that as of December 2018, North Node has just entered the sign of Cancer. McWhirter's work suggests this point of the zodiac will mark the peak of the strength of the current 18.6 year cycle which began in late 2008/early 2009. In fact, towards the end of 2018 a trade dispute with China was provoked by the occupant of the White House which had immediate effects on the economy. No surprise, given the hard 90 degree aspect between Node and Uranus that McWhirter warned about. In late 2019, Saturn and Pluto will make a 180 degree aspect to the Node, which McWhirter warns is a bad situation. Couple this with the Gann Master Cycle in 2020, and I think we can all surmise here and now that the rumblings we are hearing about a coming recession are indeed warranted. Looking farther afield, in 2026 the Node will enter Aquarius to mark the end of the 18.6 year cycle. Uranus at the time will be in Gemini and Saturn will be 90 degrees to the Node. This portends to be a very negative time as at least one other astro cycle is indicating the U.S.A. being at war. . But that is still 8 years off, so try not to worry too much. Just be aware.

4

Venus Cycles 2019

Earlier in this manuscript I touched on Venus conjunctions. Let's now take a more thorough look at Venus and its cycles.

Venus orbits the Sun in 225 days relative to an observer standing at a fixed venue like the Sun. To an observer here on Earth, a moving frame of reference, Venus appears to take 584 days to orbit the Sun. Along the way, that same observer on Earth will note periods of time when Venus is not visible in the early morning or evening sky. This is because the planet is between Earth and Sun in its orbital journey. We call this an Inferior Conjunction. As Venus slowly moves out of conjunction, it will become visible as the Morning Star. During that part of its journey when Venus is 180 degrees opposite Earth, it is said to be at Superior Conjunction. As it moves out of conjunction, it becomes visible as the Evening Star.

Venus was at Superior Conjunction on March 28, 2013 (8 Aries), October 25, 2014 (1 Scorpio), June 6, 2016 (16 Gemini) and January 8, 2018 (18 Capricorn). Venus was at Inferior Conjunction on June 6, 2012 (15 Gemini), January 11, 2014 (21 Capricorn), August 15, 2015 (22 Leo), March 25, 2017 (4 Aries), and October 26, 2018 (3 Scorpio). Plot these groups of Superior Conjunction events on a zodiac wheel. Note how they can be joined to form a 5-pointed star called a pentagram. Likewise, the Inferior Conjunction events can be plotted and joined to form a pentagram.

As Venus orbits around the Sun along the ecliptic plane, it moves above and below the plane. The high points and low points in this motion are termed declination maxima and minima. As the chart in Figure 10 illustrates, the minima points bear a close alignment to the conjunction events. As these conjunctions (or declination minima) approach, it is highly advisable to be alert for sudden market moves that could damage your investment portfolio.

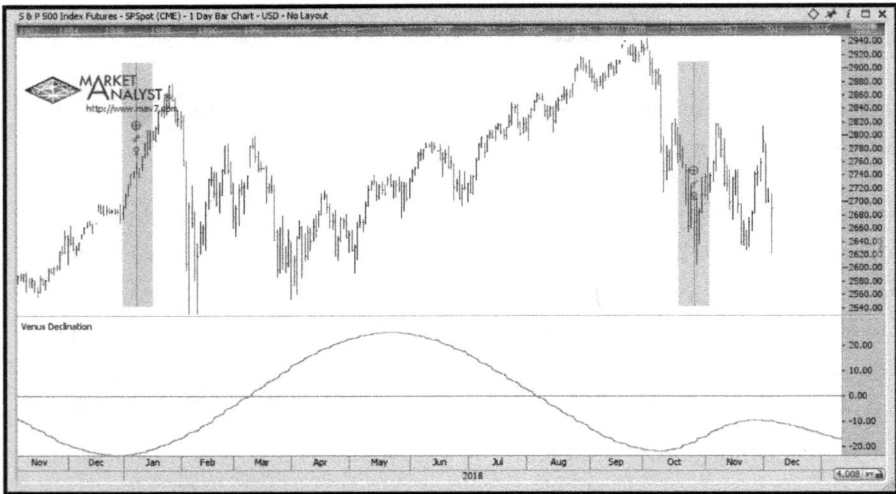

Figure 10 Venus Conjunction and Declination

However, not all declination highs and lows align to conjunctions. It is best to note the events separately.

➤ For 2019, Venus will make a declination low during most of February and again from mid-November to mid-December.

➤ There will be a Superior Conjunction event on August 14. Watch for adverse market moves on either side of this date.

Another cyclical event pertaining to Venus is retrograde. When discussing the basics of Astrology in a previous chapter, I used the analogy of race cars on a track passing each other to explain retrograde. To help understand the science of Venus retrograde, consider the diagram in Figure 11.

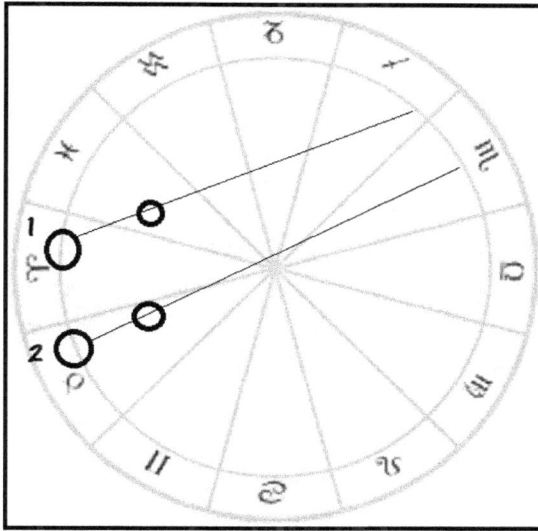

Figure 11 Venus retrograde – The Concept

In 30 days of time planet Earth (shown as the larger circles in the diagram) will travel 30 degrees of the zodiac (from point 1 to point 2). But, Venus is a faster mover. In the same 30 days of time, Venus (shown as the smaller circles) will travel through about 42 degrees of the zodiac (point 1 to point 2) – passing by Earth in the process. From our vantage point here on Earth, initially as Venus is setting up to pass Earth, we see Venus in the sign of Sagittarius. These sign determinations are made in Figure 11 by extending a line from planet Earth through Venus to the outer edge of the zodiac wheel. As Venus completes its trip past Earth, we see it in the sign of Scorpio. In other words, the way we see it here on Earth, Venus has moved backwards as it passed Earth. This is the concept of retrograde. To the ancients who did not fully understand how the cosmos worked, it must have been awe-inspiring to see a planet move backwards in the heavens relative to the constellation stars.

There is a curiously strong correlation between equity markets and Venus retrograde. Sometimes Venus retrograde events encompass a sharp market inflection point. Sometimes a market peak or bottom will follow closely behind a retrograde event, sometimes a peak or bottom will immediately precede a retrograde event. When you know a Venus retrograde event is approaching, use a suitable chart technical indicator such as DMI or Wilder Volatility Stop to determine if the price trend is changing.

Figure 12 illustrates price behavior of the S&P 500 Index during 2017 and part of 2018. Note the correlation between retrograde events and price swings. Aggressive traders can avail themselves of these retrograde correlations. Less aggressive investors may simply wish to place a stop loss order under their positions to guard against sharp price pullbacks.

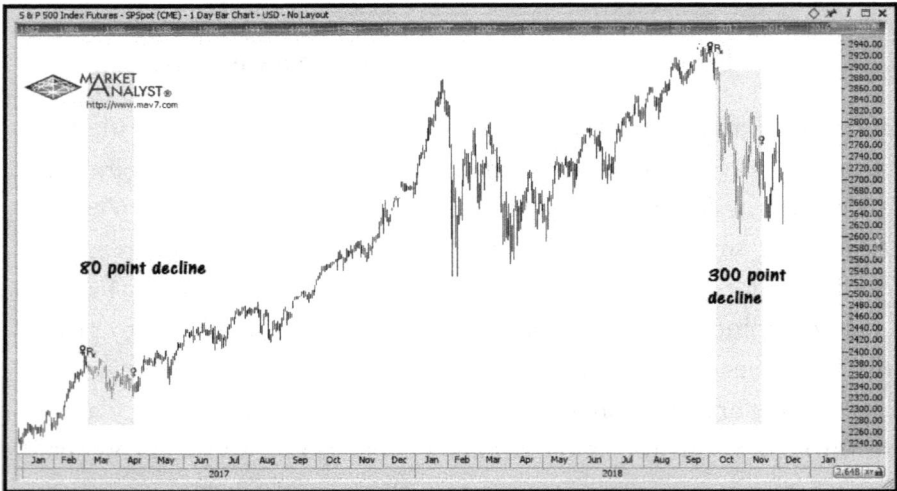

Figure 12 S&P 500 Index and Venus retrograde

As a further example, Figure 13 illustrates price performance of the S&P/ASX All Australian 200 Index. Venus retrograde events in 2017 and 2018 have been overlaid.

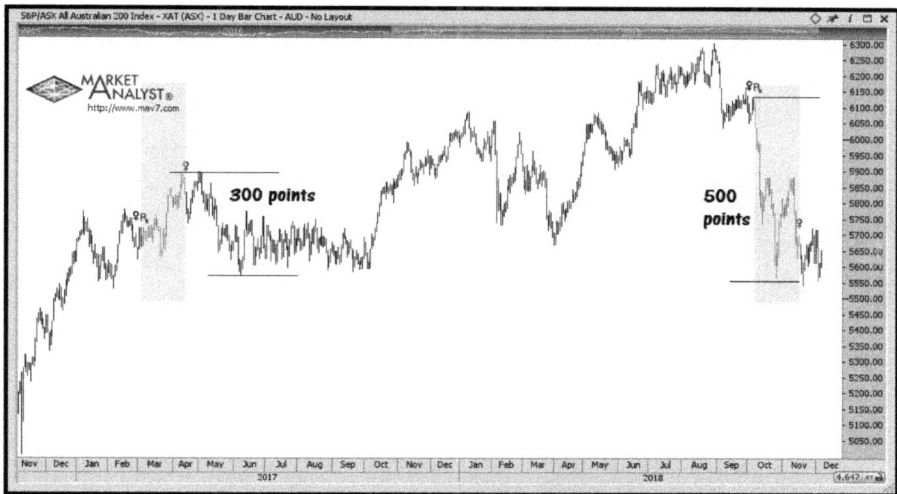

Figure 13 Venus retrograde and the ASX 200 Index

➢ There are no Venus retrograde events in 2019. Venus will again be retrograde in the May-June timeframe of 2020.

5

Mercury Cycles

Mercury is the smallest planet in our solar system. Mercury is also the closest planet to the Sun. As a result of its proximity to the powerful gravitational pull of the Sun, Mercury moves very quickly – completing one sidereal orbit of the Sun in 88 days.

Scientists at NASA have now concluded that Mercury does in fact have a di-polar magnetic field. This field is strong enough to deflect solar wind particles that have emanated from the Sun. These deflected solar winds then carry on towards the Earth. Scientists have also determined that Mercury has an eccentric orbit in which its distance from the Sun will range from 46 million kms to 70 million kms. When Mercury is *nearer* to the Sun (ie… 46 million kms away), it is moving at its fastest (~56.6 kms per second). When Mercury is *farther* from the Sun (ie… 70 million kms away), it is moving slower (~38.7 kms per second). The point where it is nearest to the Sun is called *Perihelion*. The point where it is farthest from the Sun is called *Aphelion*.

Related to Aphelion and Perihelion is the *Elongation* of Mercury. Elongation refers to the angle between a planet and the Sun, using Earth as a reference point. Figure 14 illustrates the notion of Elongation.

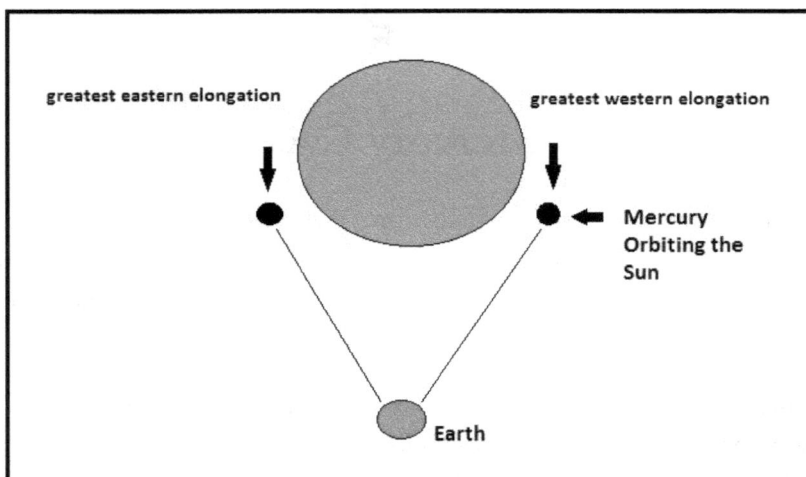

Figure 14 Elongation of Mercury

Consider that in 2018 Mercury was at its greatest easterly elongation on March 15, July 12 and November 6. Mercury was at its greatest westerly elongation on January 1, April 29, August 26 and December 15.

Figure 15 illustrates these events on a chart of the S&P 500. Sometimes these events align to the start of a rally. Other times these elongations align to the start of a decline. In any case, these dates should be anticipated closely. Mark them on your calendar.

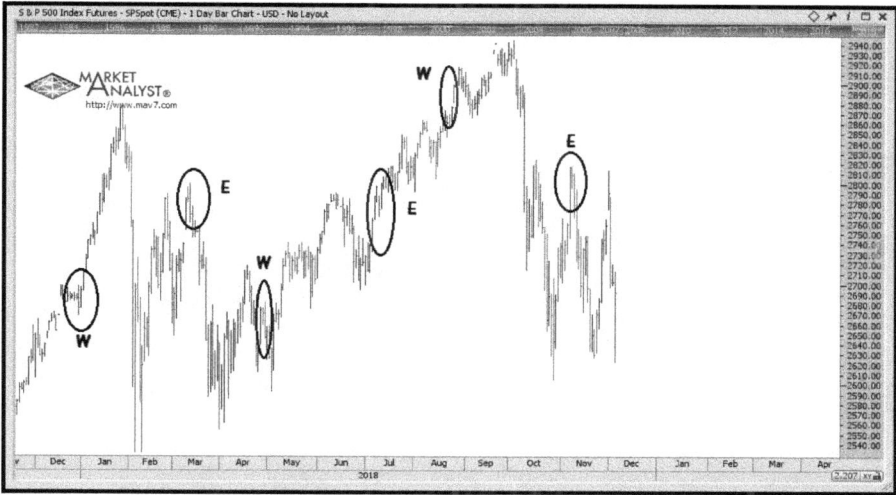

Figure 15 2018 Mercury Elongation events

> For 2019, Mercury will be at its greatest easterly elongation February 27, June 23 and October 23. It will be at greatest westerly elongation April 11, August 9 and November 28.

Along the way, in addition to times of maximum elongation there will be retrograde events. Mercury retrograde is probably one of the most potent planetary influences for investors and traders to be aware of. We all too often hear about Mercury retrograde events in mundane Astrology. Do not sign important contracts during Mercury retrograde, do not cross the street, do not leave your house and so on. While I tend to ignore this mundane talk, I have noticed a striking correlation between financial market behavior and Mercury retrograde events.

To understand the science of Mercury retrograde, consider the diagram in Figure 16.

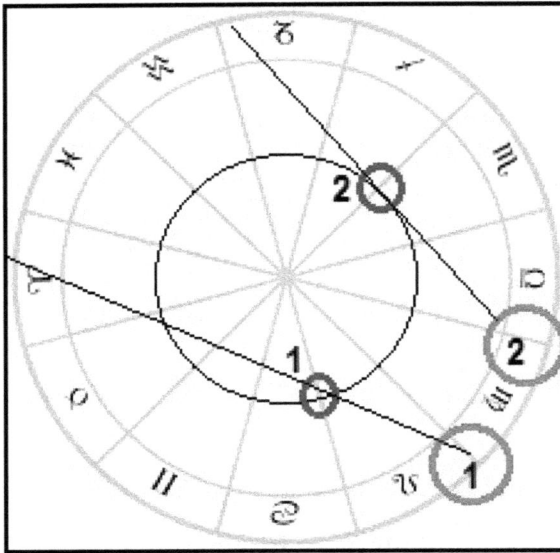

Figure 16 Mercury retrograde – The Concept

In 30 days of time planet Earth (shown as the larger circles in the diagram) will travel 30 degrees of the zodiac (from point 1 to point 2). But, Mercury is a faster mover. In the same 30 days of time, Mercury (shown as the smaller circles) will travel through about 120 degrees of the zodiac (point 1 to point 2) – passing by Earth in the process. From our vantage point here on Earth, initially as Mercury is setting up to pass Earth, we see Mercury in the sign of Aries. These sign determinations are made by extending a line from planet Earth through Mercury to the outer edge of the zodiac wheel. As Mercury completes its trip past Earth, we see it in the sign of Capricorn. In other words, the way we see it here on Earth, Mercury has moved backwards as it passed Earth. There is a curiously strong correlation between equity markets and Mercury retrograde events. Sometimes Mercury retrograde events encompass a sharp market inflection point. Sometimes a market peak or bottom will follow closely behind a retrograde event, sometimes a peak or bottom will immediately precede a retrograde event. When you know a Mercury retrograde event is approaching, use a suitable chart technical indicator such as DMI or Wilder Volatility Stop to determine if the price trend is changing.

Figure 17 illustrates some 2018 Mercury retrograde events overlaid on a chart of the S&P 500. I think you will agree that Mercury retrograde events can be highly unpredictable. Sometimes in the course of a retrograde event a market index will decline and then recover all its losses. Other times, a Mercury retrograde event will provide the alert trader to a swing low entry point for a trade. When following Mercury through its retrograde events, it is strongly advised to use shorter term charting and a good trend indicator tool.

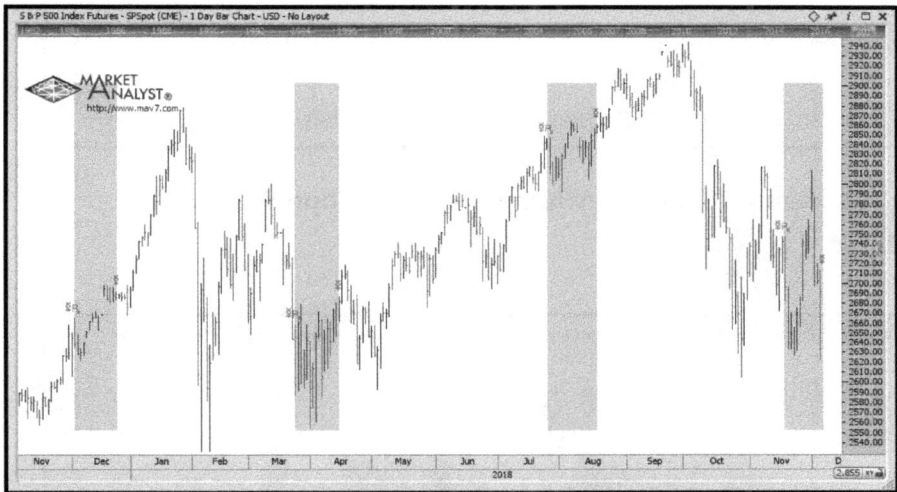

Figure 17 S&P 500 and Mercury retrograde

Mercury retrograde events can often be seen influencing commodity markets too.   Figure 18 illustrates the correlation between Copper futures prices and Mercury retrograde. While the average investor may not be aggressively trading Copper futures, this correlation could be used to better manage price risk of copper-related mining stocks in an investment portfolio.

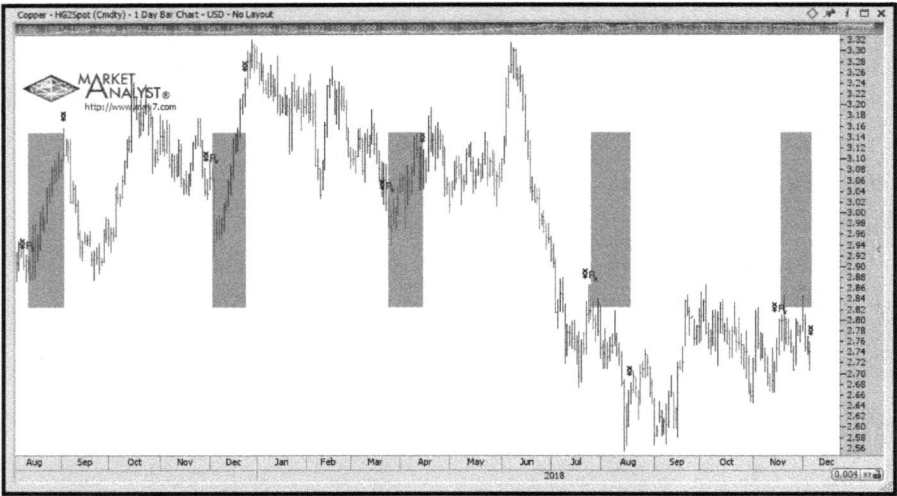

Figure 18 Mercury retrograde and Copper futures

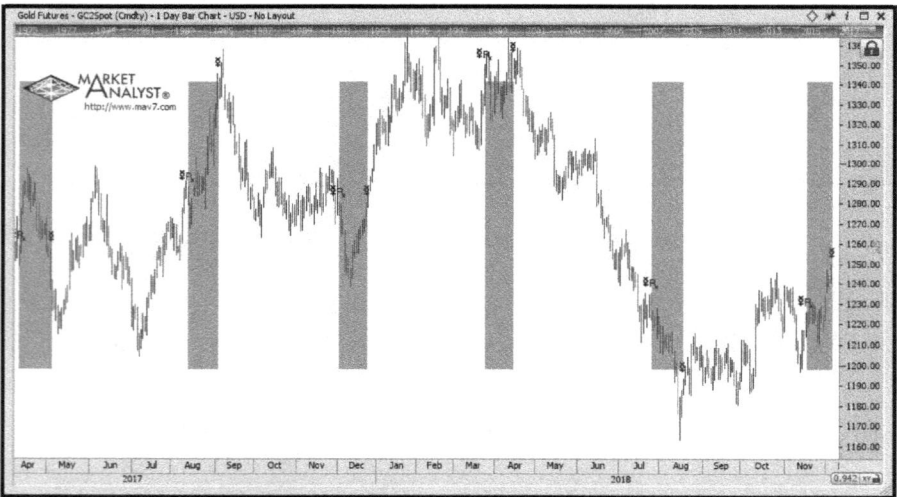

Figure 19 – Mercury retrograde and Gold futures

Figure 19 illustrates Gold futures prices overlaid with Mercury retrograde events in 2017 and 2018. Note how Mercury retrograde events align to sharp price trend swings. Traders and investors who follow Gold futures or even Gold mining stocks may wish to rely on

Mercury retrograde events when making buy and sell decisions. As I sit here finishing the final edits on this manuscript, I note that in August as retrograde was wrapping up, Gold recorded a significant low. A retrograde event has just concluded and I am now watching Gold to see whether the recent rally will fade away as well.

Whatever country you happen to reside in, check the major stock market index for that location to determine if there is a correlation to Mercury retrograde. If there is, take advantage of it. If trading or investing in stocks that are tied to a specific commodity, check to see if there is a correlation between that commodity and Mercury retrograde.

For 2019, Mercury will be:

➢ In retrograde from March 5 through March 27.

➢ In retrograde from July 7 through July 31.

➢ In retrograde from October 31 through November 19

6

Professor Weston's Cycles

Some time ago, late at night, whilst scouring the Internet looking for old Astrology manuscripts for sale, I came upon a white paper written in 1921 by a mysterious person going by the name of Professor Weston from Washington, D.C. I paid $50 for this product, and I am thrilled that I did. Never in my research travels to various libraries have I come across this name. I cannot find any other publications by him, although I understand there might be two more white papers out there somewhere. Who exactly he was, I will likely never know. Another one of those figures who emerged to write his ideas down and then vanished into the ether.

In his day, Weston analyzed copious amounts of data from the Dow Jones Average. He applied cosine Fourier mathematics and he came up with a general set of rules for the Dow. I have recently checked his model against the Dow Jones over the past number of years and I find that his model is still accurate.

I am not going to go into great elaboration here, but I will list for you his key points on the Dow Jones Index.

Perhaps Weston knew W.D. Gann. Perhaps he just knew of him. In any case, Weston followed the 20 year cycle of Jupiter and Saturn. He further broke this long cycle into two components of 10 years.

He went on to describe how investors can expect a 20 month cycle to begin in November of the 1st year of the 10 year cycle.

He said another 20 month cycle begins in November of the 5th year of the 10 year cycle.

He said 28 month cycles began in July of the 3rd and 7th years of the 10 year cycle.

A 10 month cycle begins in November of the 9th year of the 10 year cycle.

A 14 month cycle begins in September of the 10th year of the 10 year cycle.

The current Master Cycle started in June 2000. Following Weston's methodology, the first 20 month cycle would have started in November 2000 and went until July 2002. A 28 month cycle then would have gone July 2002 through November 2004. A 20 month cycle would then have followed until July 2006. A 28 month cycle then ran July 2006 through November 2008. A 10 month cycle then ran through until September 2009. Lastly, a 14 month cycle lasted until November 2010.

For the second half of the Master Cycle, year 1 would be 2010 (180 degree opposition of Saturn and Jupiter begins late in 2010 and is exact very early in 2011), year 3 would be 2012, year 5 would be 2014, year 7 will be 2016, year 9 will be 2018 and year 10 will be 2019. The next new Master Cycle will commence then in November 2020.

Put another way, the first 20 month cycle would start in November 2010 and go until July 2012. A 28 month cycle would then go July 2012 through November 2014. A 20 month cycle would then follow until July 2016. A 28 month cycle would then run July 2016 through November 2018. A 10 month cycle will then go through until September 2019. Lastly, a 14 month cycle will last until November 2020.

Weston also identified some secondary cycles within the 10 year half-Master cycles. He argued that the 16th Harmonic of a 10 year period (120 months) was actually the heliocentric periodicity of Venus. (120 x 30 / 16 = 225 days which is the time it takes Venus to orbit the Sun).

He postulated that in the various years of a 10 year cycle, there would be market maxima and minima as listed in Figure 20.

Year of Cycle	Maxima in	Maxima in
1	March	October
2		May
3	January	September
4	April	November
5	May	November
6		June
7	January	September
8		June
9	April	
10	February	August

Figure 20 Weston's Secondary Cycles

Looking closer at Weston's interval cycles, the 20 month cycle running from November 2010 through July 2012 is shown in Figure 21. The secondary maxima points have also been added to this chart in March and October 2011 and May 2012. I think we can all agree that these predicted maxima points were pretty good warning signs of market pullbacks.

Figure 21 Weston's Secondary Maxima

The 28 month cycle running through to November 2014 is illustrated in Figure 22 with secondary maxima overlaid. There was a sharp pullback in late December 2012, which should have occurred in January 2013 according to Weston's secondary maxima model. The September 2013 maxima prediction aligned to an actual pullback. The April 2014 predicted maxima came with a 600 point pullback on the Dow. The November 2014 predicted maxima was if anything about a week early as the actual pullback occurred early in December.

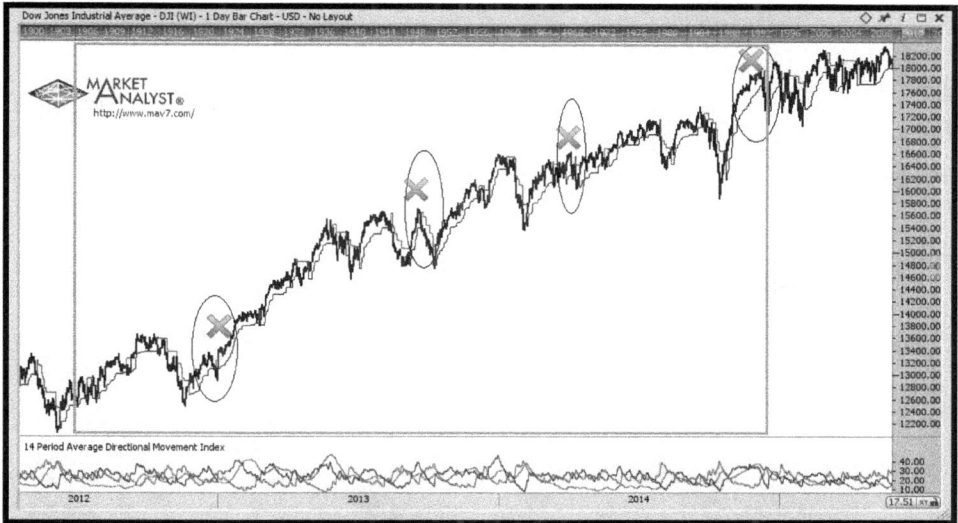

Figure 22 Weston's 28 Month Cycle

What follows next is a 20 month cycle as illustrated in Figure 23 which runs November 2014 through July 2016. The secondary maxima points have also been added for May and November 2015 and June 2016. These predicted points all seem to align to some downwards price action. A maxima point has been added for January 2017. Not more than 150 points of pullback occurred at this predicted event, but a maxima did shave nearly 80 points off the S&P 500 starting late February just ahead of a Venus retrograde event.

We have just wrapped up the 28 month cycle which Weston says runs from July 2016 to November 2018. This cycle at its end marked the Congressional mid-term elections in America. In fact, the S&P 500 recorded a swing high on November 8 and as I write this manuscript continues to struggle.

September 2017, according to Weston, should have seen a secondary maxima (it actually came in August), as should have June 2018. April 2019 and February/August 2020 should see maxima as well. In fact, mid-June 2018 marked a swing high and a loss of 100 points on the S&P 500.

A 10 month cycle will then take us to September 2019 and a 14 month cycle will take us to November 2020 and the start of a new Master Cycle. We are in these cycles now. The 10 month cycle to September 2019 will define what the markets look like for 2019.

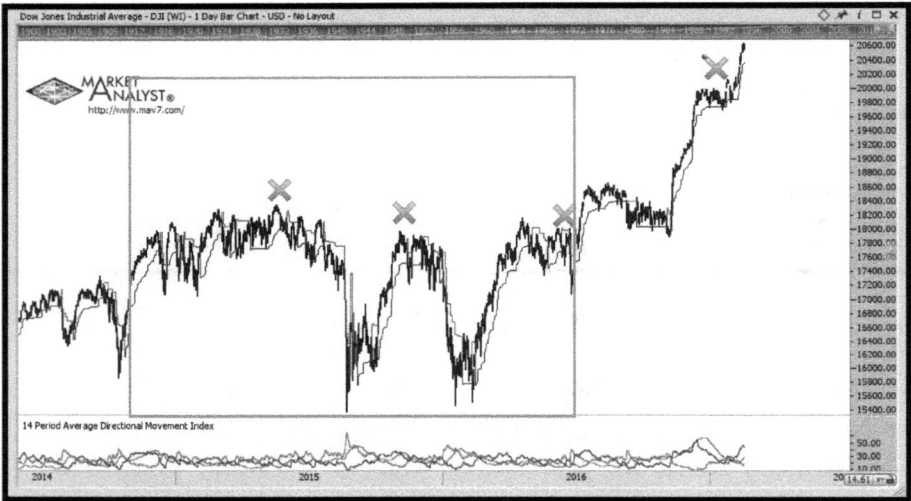

Figure 23 Weston's 20 Month Cycle

7

Shmitah and Religious Cycles

The concept of Shmitah is rooted in the Hebrew Bible.

In the book of Exodus (Chapter 23, verses 10-11), it is written:

"You may plant your land for six years and gather its crops. But during the seventh year, you must leave it alone and withdraw from it."

In the book of Leviticus (Chapter 25, verses 20-22), it is written:

"And if ye shall say: 'What shall we eat the seventh year? behold, we may not sow, nor gather in our increase'; then I will command My blessing upon you in the sixth year, and it shall bring forth produce for the three years. And ye shall sow the eighth year, and eat of the produce, the old store; until the ninth year, until her produce come in, ye shall eat the old store."

I first learned of the Shmitah when I was introduced several years ago to the writings of Rabbi Jonathan Cahn. He has done a masterful job of applying Shmitah to the paradigm of the financial markets.

Breaking these statements down into simple to understand terms means that every 7th year something will happen on the financial markets.

The first Shmita year in the modern State of Israel was 1951-52 (5712 in the Hebrew calendar). Subsequent Shmita years have been 1958–59 (5719), 1965–66 (5726), 1972–73 (5733), 1979–80 (5740), 1986–87 (5747), 1993–94 (5754), 2000–01 (5761), 2007–08 (5768), and 2014-15 (5775). The next Shmita year will be 2021-2022 (5782). A Shemitah Year starts in the month of Tishrei (the first month of the Jewish civil Calendar) and ends in the month of Elul.

The chart in Figure 24 illustrates the S&P 500 with some recent

Shmitah years overlaid. I trust you can see how the select few who understand Shmitah would have profited handsomely from these moves on the S&P 500.

Figure 24 S&P 500 and Shmitah years

The chart in Figure 25 illustrates Oil prices with Shmitah years overlaid. Again, the select few who understand Shmitah made serious money on the Crude Oil market.

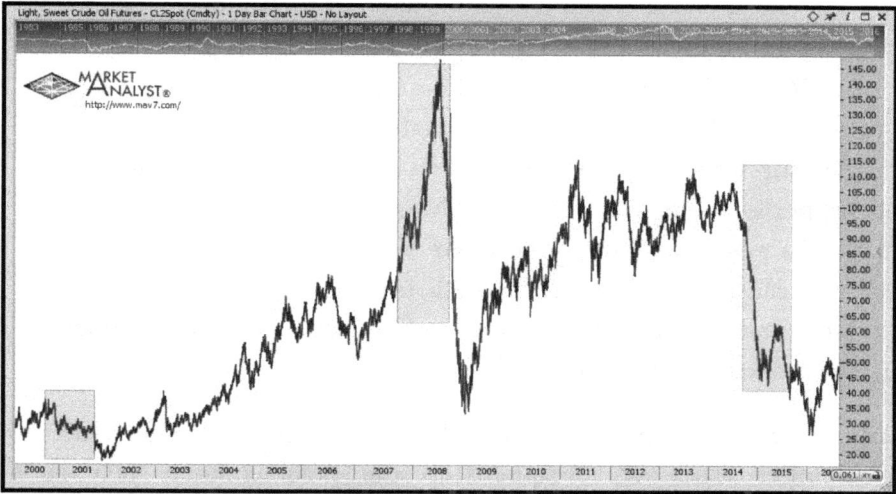

Figure 25 Crude Oil and Shmitah years

Let's now circle back to the above Biblical passages. The message is, there shall be no crop in the Shmitah year. In the year after the Shmitah, people shall live on the bounty of the crop produced in year 6 – the year immediately prior to Shmitah. In the 9th year, the newly planted crop will come in.

Figure 26 The Aftermath of Shmitah years

In Figure 26, which illustrates price action on the S&P 500, I have left a gap to represent the year following Shmitah. I have then placed another rectangle for what effectively is the second year after Shmitah Note what happens in the year immediately after Shmitah – the market actually falls and takes out the lows of the Smhitah year. But not to worry – because the Bible says we are to be living off the produce harvested (financial gains made) prior to Shmitah. Look what happens next. The market gets back its footing and starts to climb.

What are the implications for here and now? The Shmitah year ended in September 2015. We wrapped up the post Shmitah year in September 2016. Starting in the Fall of 2016, the markets regained their footing (on the heels of a Donald Trump electoral win) and started to inch higher. True, there has been volatility and uncertainty both and lots of it – driven by the various astro events outlined in this Almanac. But the trend has been to the upside. But, do not be lulled into complacency. If you decide to follow the Shmitah measure of time, take your profits in the period September 2020-2021. Plan to re-enter the markets in September 2023.

Religious cycles is a phenomenon that still requires more work on my part. What I am referring to is the notion of certain dates from the Hebrew calendar that have a strong propensity to align with swing highs and lows on the New York Stock Exchange. This notion is hinted at strongly by Rabbi Jonathan Cahn in his writings of the 7 year Shmitah cycle. Rabbi Cahn says to pay close attention to four particular dates from the Hebrew calendar.

In particular, the 1st Day of the month of Tishrei marks the start of the Jewish civil calendar, much like January 1 marks the start of the calendar that you and I follow. The 1st day of the month of Nissan marks the start of the Jewish sacred year. The 3rd important date is the 9th Day of the month of Av which marks the date when Babylon destroyed the Temple at Jerusalem in 586 BC. Other calamitous events have beset the Jewish people on the 9th of Av throughout history. In particular, Cahn tells of the mass expulsion of Jewish people from Spain in 1492. As this expulsion was going on, a certain explorer with 3 ships was about to set sail on a voyage of discovery. That explorer sailed out of port on August 3, 1492 which was one day after the 9th of Av. That explorer – indeed was Christopher Columbus and he found the New World and as Cahn tells it – that New World became a new home for the Jewish people. The 4th key date in the Jewish calendar is Shemini Atzeret (The Gathering of the Eighth Day). This date typically falls in late September through late October in the month of Tishrei. I found a helpful website at **www.chabad.org** that allows me to quickly scan back over a number of years to pick off these important dates. I have examined price action on the Dow Jones Average across several years to see what, if anything, happened at these four key dates.

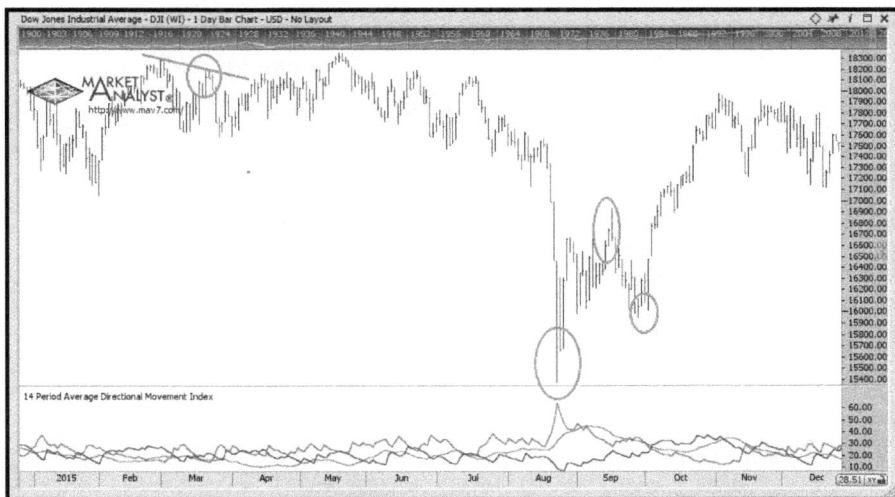

Figure 27 Key Hebrew Calendar Dates for 2015

Figure 27 has these dates circled for 2015. The 1st of Nissan aligned to a ~500 point pullback in a choppy sideways market. The 9th of Av marked a very important swing low. The 1st of Tishrei marked a swing high and the subsequent loss of ~900 points on the DOW. This sell-off ended with Shemini Atzeret which created a swing low and the basis for a powerful rally into year end.

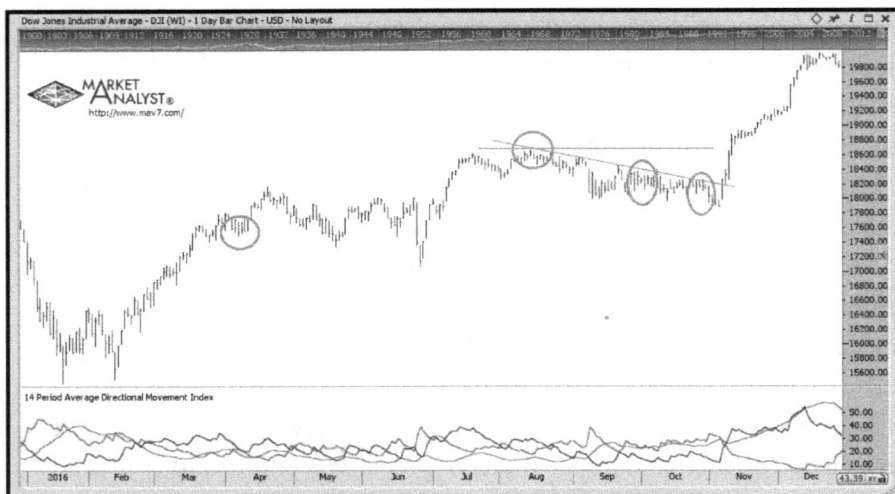

Figure 28 Key Hebrew Calendar Dates for 2016

As shown in Figure 28, the 1st of Nissan aligned to a minor perturbation in a rising market. The 9th of Av marked a high point and the start of a gradual decline on the Dow Jones Average that lead right into to the Presidential Election low point. The 1st of Tishrei showed no discernable effects in 2016. Shemini Atzeret marked the final bit of market decline into the Election low.

Back testing has shown that one should not expect such dramatic behavior each and every year, just like astrological events do not deliver stunning displays of volatility that you can set your watch by. But, these key dates should be carefully noted each year, lest they do deliver some extra volatility that a trader can take advantage of.

For 2017 the 1st of Nissan fell on March 28 and the market recorded a minor swing low before pushing higher. The 9th of Av fell on August 2 and a few days later the S&P 500 dropped 60 points. The 1st of Tishrei fell on September 21and little happened. Shemini Atzeret fell on October 12 and nothing happened.

For 2018, the 1st of Nissan fell on March 17, the 9th of Av fell on July 21, the 1st of Tishrei fell on September 10 and Shemini Atzeret fell on October 1. Figure 29 shows how the S&P 500 responded to these dates. Three of the four dates align to significant turning points. I say three because in September the market pundits were calling for a peak and a decline. But, the 1st of Tishrei fooled all of them and saw a final push higher, right into the Shemini Atzeret holiday....and then the markets fell.

Figure 29 Key Hebrew Calendar Dates for 2018

For 2019, these key Hebrew calendar dates will fall as follows:

1st of Nissan will be April 6, the 9th of Av will be August 10, the 1st of Tishrei will be September 30 and Shemini Atzeret will be October 21.

8

Synodic and Sidereal Cycles

There are *Synodic* and *Sidereal* cycles. A Sidereal cycle is one that is measured from the vantage point of the Sun. If an observer were standing on the Sun, he or she would see Venus travel around the Sun one complete time in 225 days. Mars would take 687 days. The outer planets would take much longer. In fact, Saturn would take 29.42 years, Uranus 83.75 years, Neptune 163.74 years and Pluto 245.33 years.

A Synodic cycle is measured from the vantage point of here on Earth. To an observer standing here on terra firma, the time it takes Venus to record a conjunction with Sun until that same conjunction occurs again appears to be 584 days. Mars takes 780 days from Sun/Mars conjunction to the next Sun/Mars conjunction. Saturn takes 376 days and the other outer planets 367 to 399 days.

The Sidereal cycles of the outer planets seem to bear an alignment to larger events in history. For example, the year 1776 is key to American history. Add a Neptune cycle to 1776 and one gets 1939 – when the world was on the cusp of World War 2. The American Civil War started in 1861 with the events at Fort Sumter. Add a Uranus cycle to this date and one gets to the time when World War 2 ended. Add another Uranus cycle and that takes us to 2028. Are we headed for another major conflict? Current events in the world would lead one to think so.

Venus is one planet whose Sidereal cycles intrigue me. The chart in Figure 30 illustrates price action on the S&P 500 in 2018. Using a start point of the March 2009 lows in the depths of the financial crisis, this chart has been overlaid with the ½ intervals of the 225 day sidereal cycle. Careful examination of these intervals shows that since 2009, they have landed within days of corrections on the S&P 500. True, some corrections have been minor, but some have been more significant.

For 2019, watch the time around April 18 and then every 112 days thereafter.

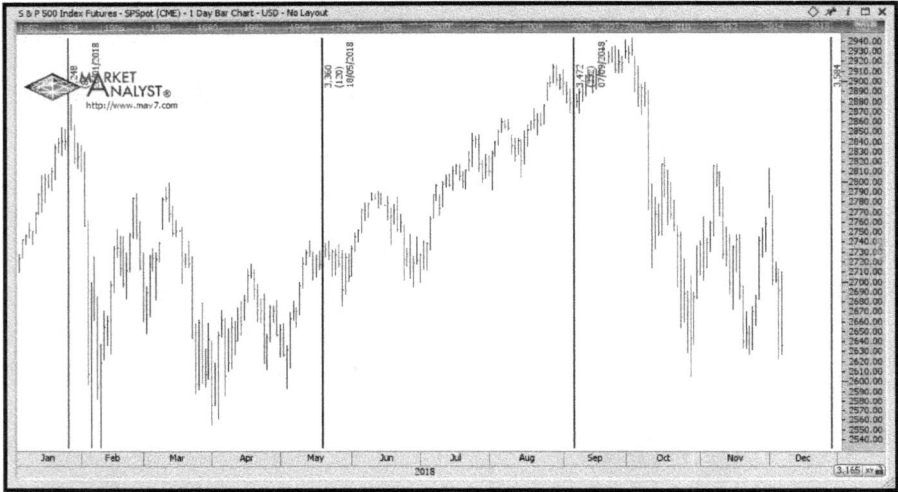

Figure 30 Venus Sidereal Cycles

Mars also fascinates me from a Synodic perspective. Using a start point of the 1987 crash (which in hindsight was a relatively minor event according to our present paradigm), one can overlay the 780 day Mars synodic cycles and their ½ measures of 390 days. Figure 31 illustrates these cycles on an S&P 500 chart dating to 2015. Sometimes these Mars intervals align to market peak turning points, sometimes to market low swing points. At the far left of the chart, a Mars interval landed atop a small downturn inflection point as did the interval in 2016. The 2017 interval played little or no role, but look at the interval that landed in October 2018 – right at a critical turning point downwards.

From October 1, 2018 count forward in 390 day intervals to identify the next timeframe to be alert to. The subject of orbital cycles is more far reaching than I have alluded to here. This area of Astrology is an ongoing work in progress for me.

Figure 31 Mars Synodic Cycles

The Moon also has cycles of interest. The sidereal period of the Moon is 27.5 days and the synodic period is 29.53 days. This latter period is where we get the expression 'lunar month'. During each sidereal lunar cycle, the Moon can be seen to vary in its position above and below the lunar ecliptic. In other words, in a sidereal period, the Moon will go from maximum declination to maximum declination. Note the regular periodicity of the pattern. It is said that W.D. Gann was a proponent of following lunar cycles when trading Soybeans and Cotton. And why not? After all, the Moon and its gravitational pull is largely responsible for the ocean tides. Our bodies are substantially water, so it stands to reason that the Moon will influence our behaviors which in turn will affect the markets.

Figure 32 presents a plot of Moon declination for 2018.

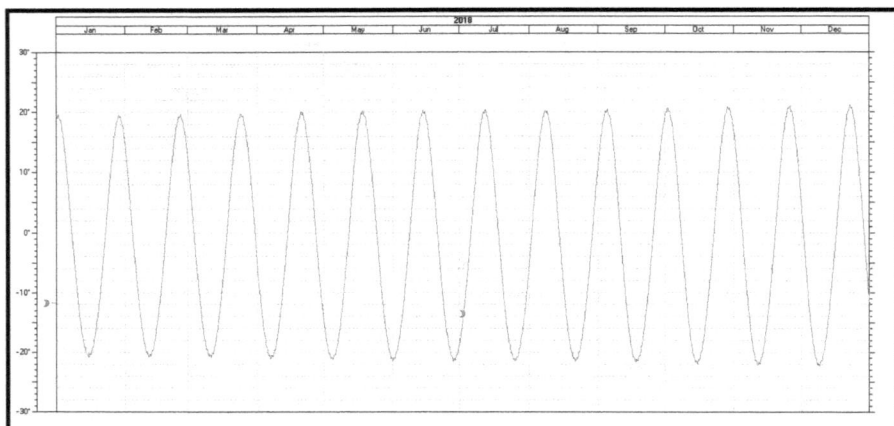

Figure 32 Moon Declination 2018

Take a look at a daily chart of a stock you like to trade or invest in. Take a look at a commodity futures contract you follow. You will often find that at times of maximum or minimum lunar declination there will be a short term change in price behavior best witnessed on an hourly chart setup.

To assist you in some back-testing of your own, consider that in 2017, Moon recorded maximums in its declination on January 11, February 8, March 7, April 3, April 30, May 27, June 25, July 21,August 18, September 14, October 11, November 8 and December 6.

To further assist you, consider that in 2017, Moon recorded minimums in declination on January 24, February 22, March 21, April 17, May 15, June 11, July 8, August 5, September 1, September 28, October 26, November 22 and December 20.

For 2018, Moon recorded maximums in its declination on January 2, January 29, February 26, March 25, April 22, May 19, June 15, July 12, August 9, September 5, October 2, October 30, November 26 and December 23.

For 2018, Moon recorded minimums in its declination on January 16, February 12, March 11, April 7, May 5, June 1, June 28, July 26, August 22, September 18, October 16, November 12 and December 9.

For 2018, Moon passed 0 degrees of declination on January 8 and 23, February 5, and 20, March 4, 19 and 31, April 15 and 28, May 12 and 25, June 9 and 21, July 6 and 18, August 2, 15 and 29, September 11 and 26, October 9 and 23, November 5 and 19, December 2, 17 and 30.

To illustrate, the chart in Figure 33 illustrates Soybean futures prices during 2018. I have overlaid the chart with a dark vertical line at those lunar declination events that do align to short term trend changes. Note that sometimes, the point of zero declination aligns to a trend change.

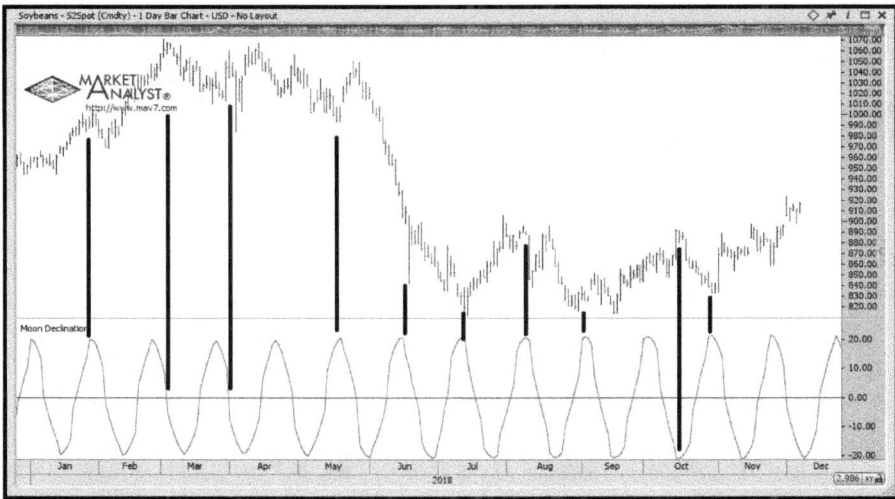

Figure 33 Moon Geocentric Declination and Soybeans

Figure 34 illustrates Cotton futures prices during 2018. I have overlaid the chart with a dark vertical line at those lunar declination events that do align to short term trend changes.

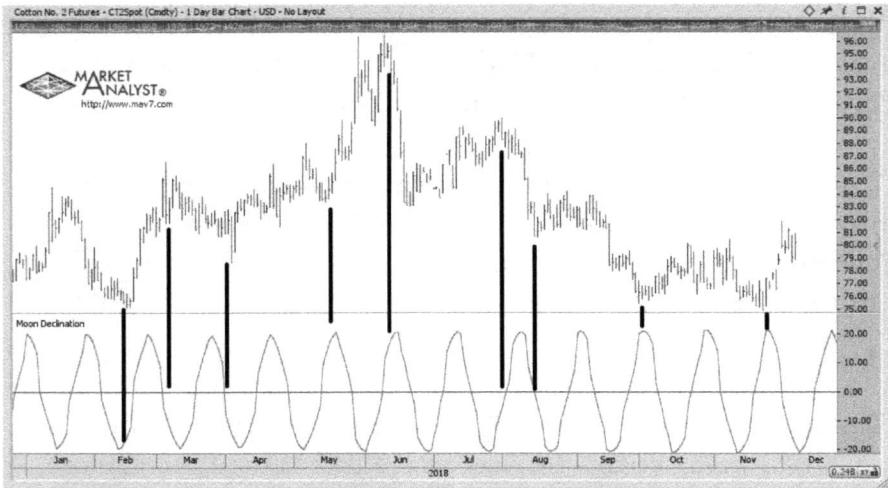

Figure 34 Moon Geocentric Declination and Cotton

➢ For 2019, Moon will record maximums in its declination on January 20,   February 16, March 15, April 12, May 9, June 5, July 2, July 30, August 26, September 23, October 19, November 17 and December 14.

➢ For 2019, Moon will record minimums in its declination on February 2, March 1, March 28, April 26, May 22, June 19, July 17, August 13, September 8, October 5, November 2, November 30, and December 27.

➢ For 2019, Moon will pass 0 degrees of declination on January 26, February 10 and 22, March 8 and 21, April 5 and 19, May 2, 15 and 30, June 12 and 25, July 9 and 22, August 5 and 20, September 1, 16 and 28, October 13 and 27, November 8 and 23, and December 7 and 19.

9

Parallel and Contra Parallel

As has been discussed, as the various celestial bodies make their respective journeys around the Sun, they can be seen to move relative to our vantage point of the celestial equator. Declination refers to this positioning of a celestial body above or below the celestial equator plane. Celestial bodies experience declinations of up to about 25 degrees above and below the celestial equator plane.

Declination can be viewed one planet at a time or by pairs of planets. Let's suppose that at a particular time Mars can be seen as being 10 degrees of declination above the celestial equator and at that same time Venus is also at 10 degrees of declination. Let's further suppose that we allow for up to 1.5 degrees tolerance in our measurement of declinations. We would say these two planets were at *parallel declination*. Let's take another example and suppose that at a given time Jupiter was at 5 degrees of declination above the celestial equator and at that same time period Pluto was at 6.5 degrees declination below the celestial equator. Again, let's allow for up to 1.5 degrees of tolerance. We would say that Jupiter and Pluto were at *contra-parallel declination*. As this Almanac will show, parallel and contra-parallel events have a powerful bearing on certain aspects of the financial markets.

I have spent many hours exploring parallel and contra-parallel events with respect to commodity futures contracts. This research was spurred on by a 25 year old Astrology book I found in a used bookshop in early 2017. In studying this old book, I have found there are *some* commodities that in fact bear a correlation to parallel and contra-parallel conditions that were in place at the First Trade date. I strongly suggest using these parallel and contra-parallel events in combination with the other Astrology events outlined throughout this book. Using a suitable software program or possibly a reliable on-line source, obtain the planetary declinations at the first trade date for the stock or commodity in question. Examine the data for evidence of parallel and contra parallel events. Watch for these parallel and contra-parallel occurrences to repeat themselves at future dates. These dates may align to short term trend changes. To illustrate, the following Gold, Cotton, Crude Oil, and Soybeans studies show you how it is done. This is still very much a work in progress for me and much remains to be studied yet.

Gold

Gold futures started trading in New York on Dec 31, 1974. At that date, the planets were at the following declinations relative to the ecliptic:

Sun	-23.06 degrees
Venus	-22.42 degrees
Mars	-22.45 degrees
Jupiter	-7.39 degrees
Saturn	+22.05 degrees
Uranus	-11.37 degrees
Neptune	-20.3 degrees
Pluto	+11.44 degrees

Looking closer at these numbers we can see the following:

Uranus is contra-parallel to Pluto (contra-parallel = declinations within 1.5 degrees of each other, but signs are opposite)

Saturn is contra-parallel Mars

Saturn is contra-parallel Venus

Saturn is contra-parallel Sun

Mars is parallel Sun (parallel = declinations with 1.5 degrees of each other, signs are the same)

Mars is parallel Venus

Sun is parallel Venus

The price chart of Gold in Figure 35 has been overlaid with some of these events from 2018. I find it curiously interesting how these events all too often align to steep price moves and trend changes.

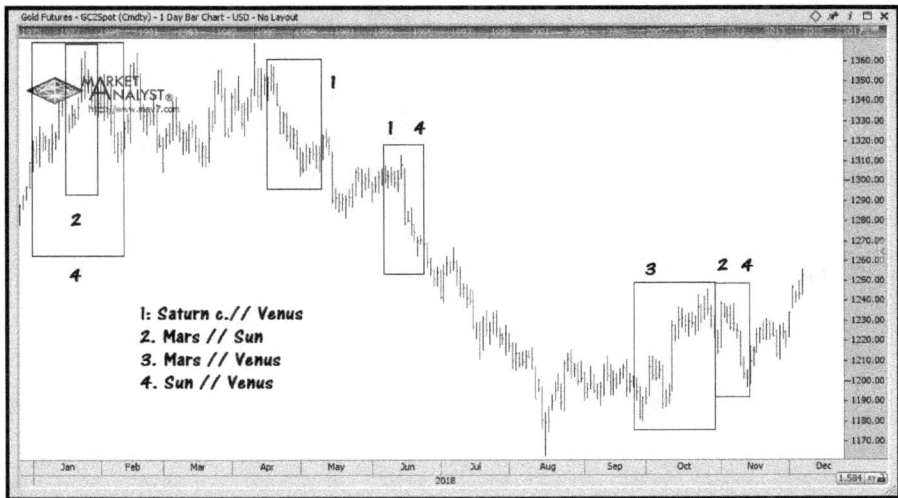

Figure 35 Gold and Declination Phenomenon

For 2019, Mars will be parallel Sun from June 4 to 24 and again August 13 to September 6.

For 2019, Mars will be parallel Venus from June 17 to July 4 and August 15 to September 2.

For 2019, Sun will be parallel Venus June 22 to July 15, August 15 to September 2, December 10 to 20.

For 2019, Saturn will be contra-parallel Sun from May 24 through July 18.

For 2019, Saturn will be contra-parallel Venus from June 14 to July 30.

Cotton

Cotton futures started trading in New York on June 20, 1870. At that date, the planets were at the following declinations relative to the ecliptic:

Sun	+23.45 degrees
Venus	+14.84 degrees
Mars	+21.42 degrees
Jupiter	+21.32 degrees
Saturn	-22.09 degrees
Uranus	+22.31 degrees
Neptune	+6.86 degrees
Pluto	+2.99 degrees

Looking closer at these numbers we can see the following:

Sun is contra-parallel to Saturn

Sun is parallel Uranus

Saturn is contra-parallel Uranus

Uranus is parallel Jupiter

Uranus is parallel Mars

Mars is parallel Jupiter

Mars is contra-parallel Saturn

Mars is parallel Uranus

The price chart of Cotton in Figure 36 has been overlaid with some of these events from 2018. Notice how the price spike in June came during a Sun contra-parallel Saturn event.

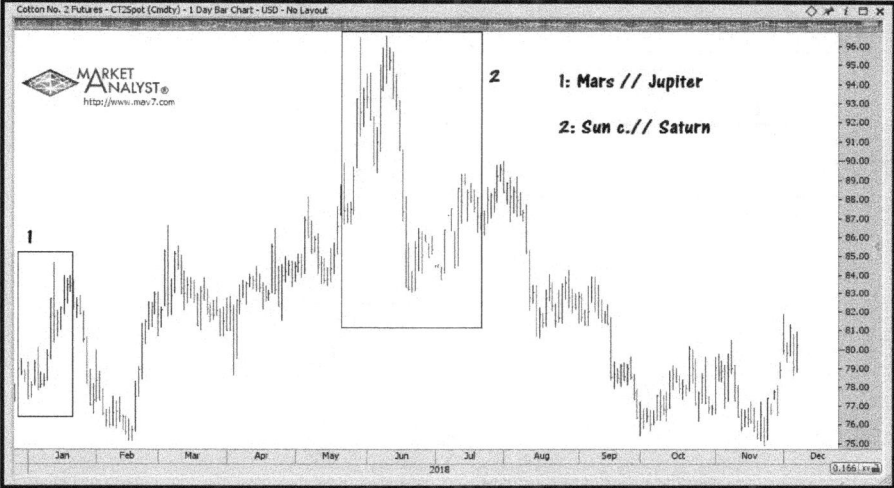

Figure 36 Cotton and Declination Phenomenon

For 2019, Saturn will be contra-parallel Sun from May 28 through July 19.

For 2019 Sun will be parallel Uranus from April 14 to April 25.

2019 will see no Saturn contra parallel Uranus events.

2019 will see no Uranus parallel Jupiter events.

2019 will see Uranus parallel Mars from February 4 to 17 and August 7 to 23.

In 2019, Mars will be contra parallel Saturn from April 7 through July 5.

Crude Oil

Crude Oil futures started trading in America on March 30, 1983. At that date, the planets were at the following declinations relative to the ecliptic:

Sun	+3.52 degrees
Venus	+16.28 degrees
Mercury	+4.38
Mars	+9.52 degrees
Jupiter	-21.18 degrees
Saturn	-9.87 degrees
Uranus	-21.70 degrees
Neptune	-22.20 degrees
Pluto	+5.42 degrees

Looking closer at these numbers we can see the following:

Sun is parallel to Pluto (declinations within 2 degrees of each other, signs are the same)

Sun is parallel Mercury

Mars is contra-parallel Saturn

Uranus is parallel Jupiter

Uranus is parallel Neptune

Jupiter is parallel Neptune

The price chart of Crude Oil in Figure 37 has been overlaid with some of these events from 2018. Note how so many price swings and inflections coincide with these declination events, especially the Mercury events.

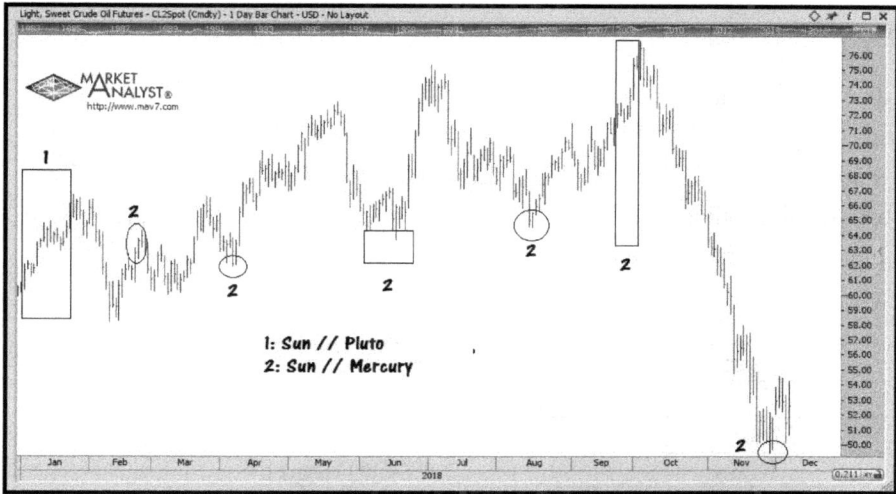

Figure 37 Crude Oil and Declination Phenomenon

For 2019, Sun will be parallel Pluto from January 1 to January 23 and again from Nov 27 to year end.

There will be one large Mars contra-parallel Saturn events in 2019 from April 1 through July 4.

There will be numerous Sun parallel Mercury events in 2019 including February 3 to 9, March 15 to 21, May 17 to 23, June 14 to 20, July 31 to August 5, September 5 to 11, November 8 to 14, and December 20 to 24.

Soybeans

As discussed in a coming chapter, the Chicago Board of Trade was founded April 3, 1848. Looking at Soybean futures through the lens of this date as opposed to the 1936 date when Soybean futures actually started trading yields some interesting finds. At the 1848 date, the planets were at the following declinations relative to the ecliptic:

Sun	+5.35 degrees
Venus	-7.26 degrees
Mercury	-6.10
Mars	+24.80 degrees
Jupiter	+23.26 degrees
Saturn	-6.08 degrees
Uranus	+6.48 degrees
Neptune	-11.48 degrees
Pluto	-5.46 degrees

Sun is parallel Uranus

Sun is contra parallel Pluto, Venus, Mercury and Saturn

Mercury is parallel Saturn

Mercury is contra parallel Uranus

Mars is parallel Jupiter

The price chart of Soybeans in Figure 38 has been overlaid with some of these events from 2018. Figure 31 illustrates how the big price collapse pertaining to the trade tiff with China came as Sun was contra parallel to Saturn.

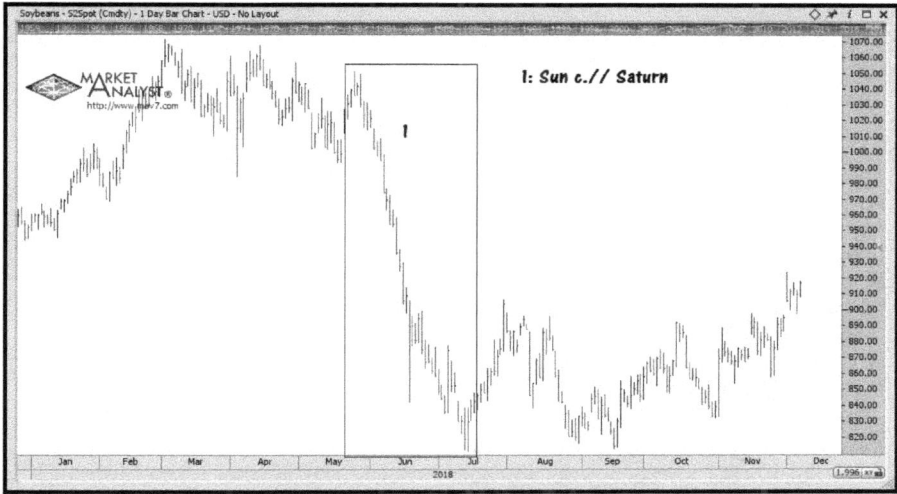

Figure 38 Soybeans (1848) and Declination Phenomenon

In 2019, Sun will be parallel Uranus April 14 to 25.

In 2019, Sun will be contra parallel Saturn from May 28 to July 19.

Mars will be parallel Jupiter from December 26, 2017 through January 17, 2018 and again from October 16 through 28.

Sun will be contra-parallel Pluto May 20 to June 11 and again June 29 through July 21st.

10

New York Stock Exchange 2019 Astrology

The brief introduction to Louise McWhirter in an earlier chapter opens the door to a look at the Astrology of the New York Stock Exchange. During her lifetime, Louise McWhirter focused intently on the Astrology of the New York Exchange and her technique which revolves around the New Moon (lunation) remains viable to this day.

The Lunation and the New York Stock Exchange

A *lunation* is the astrological term for a New Moon. At a lunation, the Sun and Moon are separated by 0 degrees which means the Sun and Moon are together in the same sign of the zodiac. The correlation between the monthly lunation event and New York Stock Exchange price movements was first popularized in 1937 by McWhirter. In her book, *Theory of Stock Market Forecasting*, she discussed how a lunation making hard aspects to planets such as Mars, Jupiter, Saturn and Uranus was indicative of a coming month of volatility on the New York Stock Exchange. She also paid close attention to Mars and Neptune - the two planets that *rule* the New York Stock Exchange. McWhirter said those times of a lunar month when the transiting Moon makes 0 degree aspects to Mars and Neptune should be watched carefully. The concept of planetary rulership extends back into the 1800s. McWhirter arrived at this rulership conclusion by observing that the 10th House of the 1792 birth horoscope wheel for the NYSE spans Pisces and Aries. Neptune rules Pisces and Mars rules Aries.

New York Stock Exchange – First Trade Chart

The New York Stock Exchange officially opened for business on May 17, 1792. As the following horoscope in Figure 39 shows, the NYSE has its Ascendant (Asc) at 14 degrees Cancer and its Mid-Heaven (MC) at 24 Pisces.

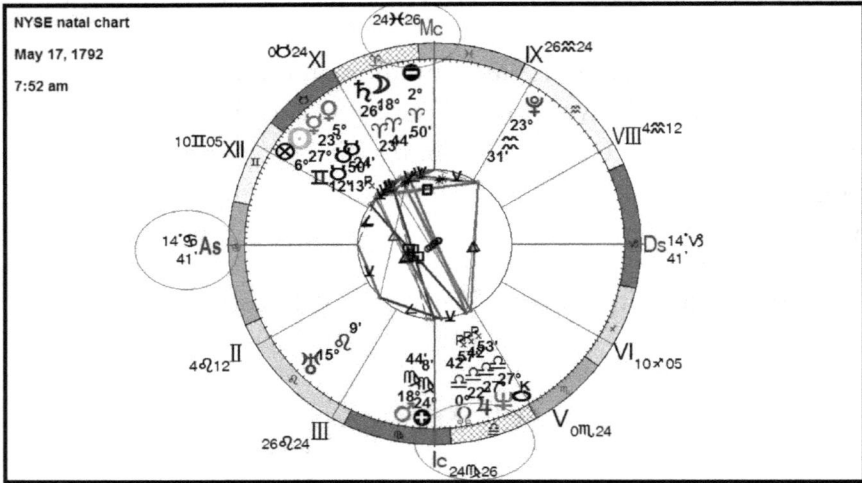

Figure 39 NYSE First Trade horoscope

McWhirter further paid close attention to those times in the monthly lunar cycle when the transiting Moon passed by the NYSE natal Asc and MC locations at 14 Cancer and 24 Pisces respectively.

Horoscope Charts and the McWhirter Methodology

In my research and writing, I follow the McWhirter methodology. When forecasting whether or not a coming month will be volatile or not for the NYSE, the McWhirter methodology starts with creating a horoscope chart for the New Moon date and positioning the Ascendant of the chart at 14 degrees Cancer - which is the Ascendant position on the 1792 natal chart of the New York Stock Exchange. Positioning the Ascendant is made easy in the Solar Fire Gold software program. Aspects to the lunation are then studied. If the lunation is at a 0, 90 or 120 degree aspect to Mars, Neptune, 14 Cancer or 24 Pisces, one can expect a volatile month ahead. A lack of such aspects portends a less volatile period. Using Solar Fire Gold I then advance the horoscope forward one day at a time watching where Moon is at each day. Aspects of the Moon to Mars, Neptune, 14 Cancer or 24 Pisces represent dates of potential trend reversals. I further pay attention to those dates when Moon is at either maximum or minimum declination. I keep in mind those dates when Mercury is retrograde and those dates when Venus is at or near its maximum or minimum declination. When I see multiple overlapping events I pay extremely close attention.

Similarly, when studying an individual stock or an individual commodity futures contract, the McWhirter approach calls for the creation of a horoscope chart at the First Trade date of the stock or commodity. The Ascendant is then shifted so that the Sun is at the Ascendant. Again, the software program Solar Fire Gold is very good for generating First Trade horoscope charts for McWhirter analysis where the Ascendant needs to be shifted.

In stock and commodity analyses, McWhirter then paid strict attention to those times of a calendar year when transiting Sun, Mars, Jupiter, Saturn, Neptune and Uranus made hard 0,90 and 180 degree aspects to the natal Mid-Heaven, natal Ascendant, natal Sun, natal Jupiter and even the natal Moon of the individual stock or commodity future being studied.

What one must be alert for at these aspects is the possibility of a trend change, the possibility of increased volatility within a trend or even the possibility of a breakout from a chart consolidation pattern. Evidence of such trend changes will be found by watching price action relative to moving averages and by utilizing oscillator type functions (MAC-D, DMI, RSI and so on). This Almanac assumes that the reader is reasonably well versed in chart technical analysis.

McWhirter Lunation Examples

The following two examples of the McWhirter method are taken from the prior versions of the Financial Astrology Almanac.

January 2016

The New Moon in January occurs on the 9ᵗʰ with Sun at 19 degrees Capricorn. Starting January 29 and continuing to February 14, Sun will be 90 degrees hard aspect to Mars . This infers increased volatility.

The chart of the S&P 500 in Figure 40 illustrates what happened during this lunar cycle. The entire lunar cycle is depicted by the price bars in the box overlaid on the chart. Note the volatility as suggested by the McWhirter analysis. The arrow in the box points to the January 29 date, the specific date that the analysis suggested to expect increased volatility.

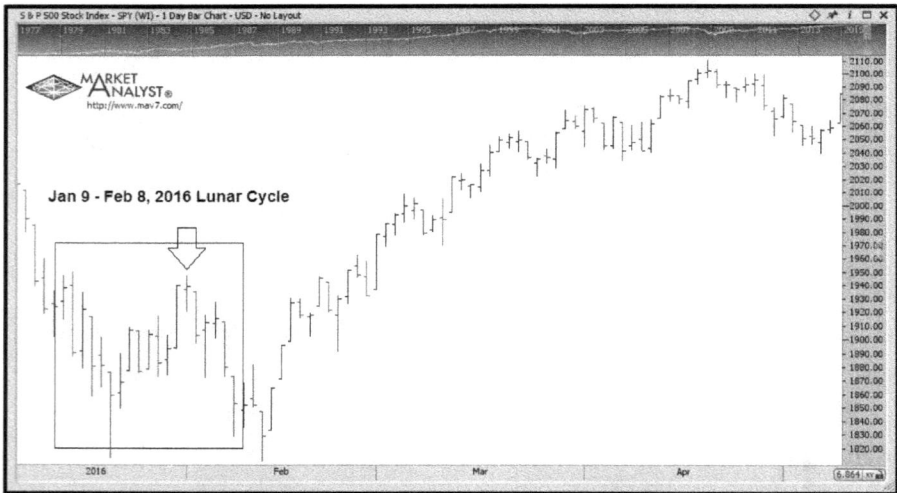

Figure 40 Lunation Event of January, 2016

July 2017

The New Moon for the July lunar cycle on the 24th of June with Sun at 2 degrees Cancer.

The lunar cycle commencing at this New Moon will run until July 23, 2017. There are no aspects between the lunation and other planets. However, there is plenty of other evidence for added volatility.

Key dates to be alert to during this lunation include:

June 24: Moon transits past NYSE co-ruler Mars which so happens to be passing the NYSE natal Asc point of 14 Cancer. This is a week-end so watch for a market reaction on the Monday. This could be a significant inflection point on the NYSE. Mars also completing its maximum declination point at this time.

June 30-July 10: Sun makes a 90 degree hard aspect to Jupiter.

July 13: Moon transits past NYSE co-ruler Neptune.

July 14: Moon passes NYSE Mid-Haven at 24 Pisces.

The chart of the S&P 500 in Figure 41 illustrates what happened during this lunar cycle. The S&P 500 posted an interim top just ahead of this lunation cycle. Weakness than set in, but a trend change occurred as Sun made its 90 degree hard aspect to Jupiter. The period July 13-14 was particularly volatile as Moon passed by co-ruler Neptune and also the Mid-Heaven. The net result of this lunar cycle was a gain by the S&P 500 , but as McWhirter's method insinuated, there was volatility along the way.

Figure 41 Lunation Event of July, 2017

January 2018

The nearest New Moon for February, 2018 occurs on the 16th of January with Sun at 26 degrees Capricorn. The lunar cycle commencing at this New Moon will run until February 15, 2018. About the only hard aspect apparent is a 90 degree square to Uranus. This stands to be over-shadowed by the more positive 0 degree aspect between the New Moon and Venus. Expect a generally positive lunar cycle.

Key dates to be alert to during this lunation include:

January 16: Moon at minimum declination.

January 20: Moon transits past NYSE co-ruler Neptune.

January 21-22: Moon transits past NYSE Mid-Heaven at 24 Pisces.

January 25: ECB Monetary Council meeting.

January 29: Moon at maximum declination.

January 29: Moon transits past the natal Ascendant point of 14 Cancer.

January 30-31: FOMC Federal Reserve Meeting.

February 9: Moon transits past co-ruler Mars.

February 12: Moon at minimum declination.

The chart of the S&P 500 in Figure 42 illustrates what happened during this lunar cycle. As the Moon transited past the critical point at 14 Cancer, the market took a sudden dive. However, it did recover and at the end of this lunar cycle had nearly recouped its losses. This example illustrates that even though a McWhirter analysis may portend a generally favorable lunar cycle, a key date within the cycle can create havoc. Thus, it is critical to follow the dates with a cycle carefully and always be sure to trail positions with a stop loss in case extreme volatility breaks out.

Figure 42 Lunation Event of January, 2018

2019 Lunation Forecasts

January 2019

Key Dates

The New Moon cycle for January, 2019 commences on the 6th of January with Sun at 15 degrees Capricorn. The horoscope in Figure 43 depicts planetary placements hours before the New Moon event itself as the Ascendant passes 14 Cancer.

The lunation has a favorable 60 degree aspect to Neptune, one of the NYSE co-rulers. But, Neptune and Mars are straddling the natal mid-Heaven point of 24 Pisces and the lunation is 180 degrees opposite the 14 Cancer point. Mars and heavy-weight Uranus are in the 10th House which is a negative force. Pluto is within orb of being conjunct the lunation which is another negative. From this arrangement, it is fair to expect a somewhat less than robust overall market during this lunation cycle.

Key dates to be alert to during this lunation include:

January 6: Moon at minimum declination.

January 10: Moon passes NYSE co-ruler Neptune.

January 11: Moon passes NYSE natal mid-Heaven point of 24 Pisces.

January 12: Moon passes NYSE co-ruler Mars. This is a Saturday, so watch for a reaction on the Friday or the following Monday.

January 17-19: Moon will make a 90 degree aspect to Neptune and Mars over this period. Moon will then make a trine (120 degree) aspect to Moon. Moon also passes the critical 14 of Cancer point. Moon will be at maximum declination as well. This overlapping group of occurrences in this short span of time could be a significant turning point on the overall market trend.

January 21: Moon makes a 120 degree aspect to Mars

January 23-24: Moon is opposite Neptune as the ECB meets.

January 25: Moon is opposite Mars.

January 29-30: Moon is 90 degrees to Neptune as the FED meets.

February 1: Moon at minimum declination.

February 2: Moon is 90 degrees to Mars.

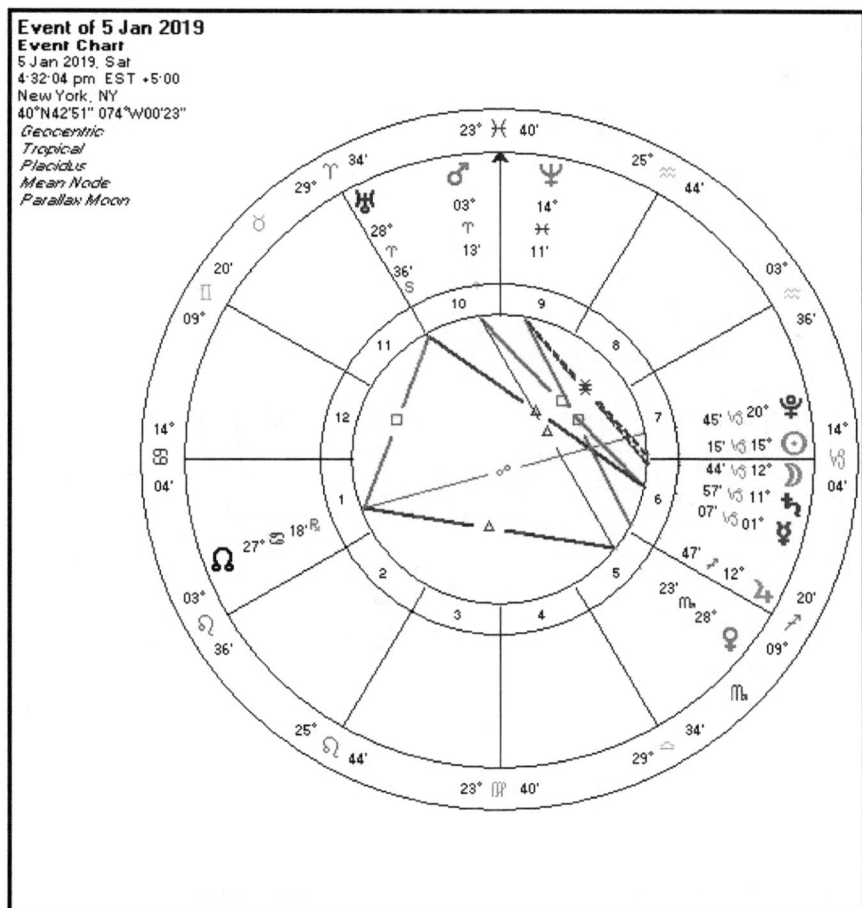

Figure 43 New Moon January 6, 2019

February 2019

Key Dates

The New Moon cycle for February, 2019 commences on the 4th of February with Sun at 15 Aquarius. The horoscope in Figure 44 depicts planetary placements just before the New Moon event itself as the Ascendant passes 14 Cancer.

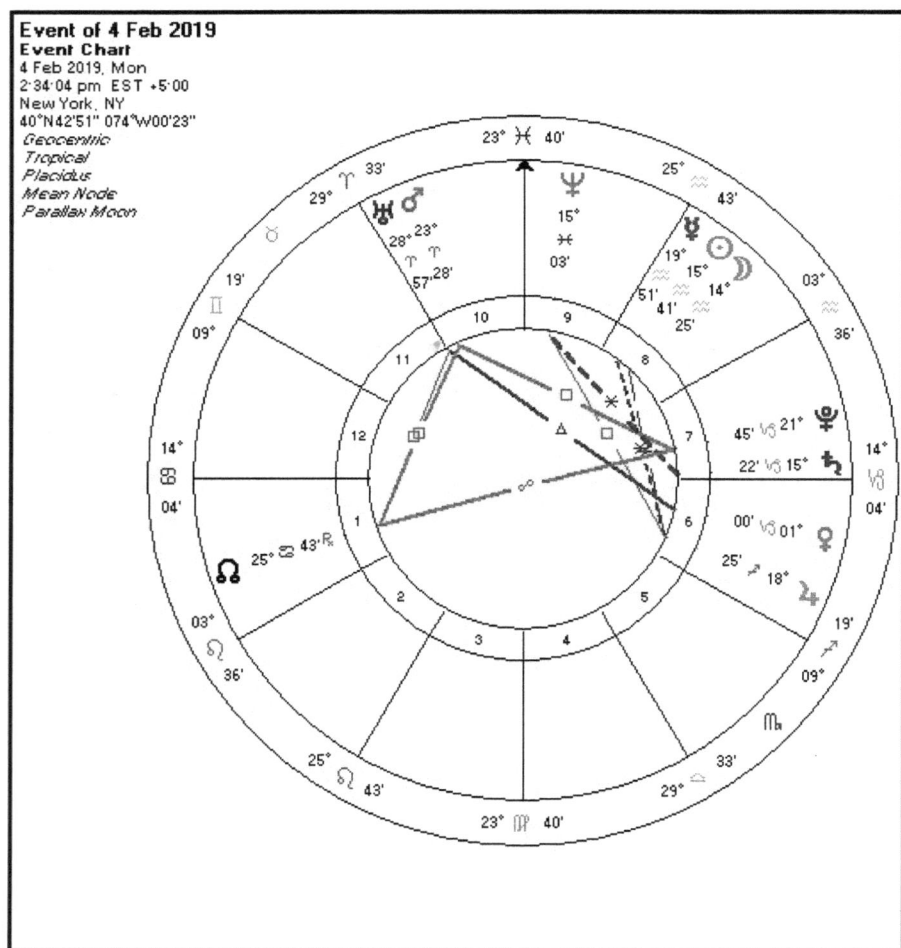

Figure 44 New Moon February 4, 2019

The lunation makes a favorable 60 degree aspect to Jupiter and a soft 30 degree aspect to ruler Neptune. Mars and Uranus are in the 10th House with Mars at the apex of a T-square formation. The 7th House contains Saturn and Pluto, with Saturn at a soft 60 degrees to ruler Neptune. This all is suggestive of a month where the trend from the prior month continues.

Key dates to be alert to during this lunation include:

February 7: Moon passes NYSE co-ruler Neptune and the 24 Pisces natal mid-Heaven location of 24 Pisces.

February 10: Moon passes NYSE co-ruler Mars. This is a Sunday, so expect a reaction on the Monday. Venus will record an declination minimum at this time, but allowing for a couple degrees of declination, the entire minima will extend out over +/- 10 days. This could align to a trend change on the markets.

February 14: Moon is 90 degrees Neptune.

February 16-17: Moon at maximum declination. Moon passes the key point of 14 Cancer. Moon is 90 degrees Mars. This is a weekend, so expect a reaction either on the Friday or the following Monday.

February 19-20: Moon is 120 degrees to Mars and then passes 180 degrees opposite Neptune.

February 23-26: Moon passes 180 degrees to Mars and 90 degrees to Neptune.

February 27-28: Mercury at maximum eastern elongation and Moon at minimum declination. This time span could present a trend change.

March 1-3: Moon at minimum declination and passing 90 degrees to Mars.

March 2019

Key Dates

The New Moon cycle for March 2019 commences on the 6th of March with Sun at 15 degrees Pisces. The horoscope in Figure 45 depicts planetary placements just hours after the New Moon as the Ascendant passes 14 Cancer.

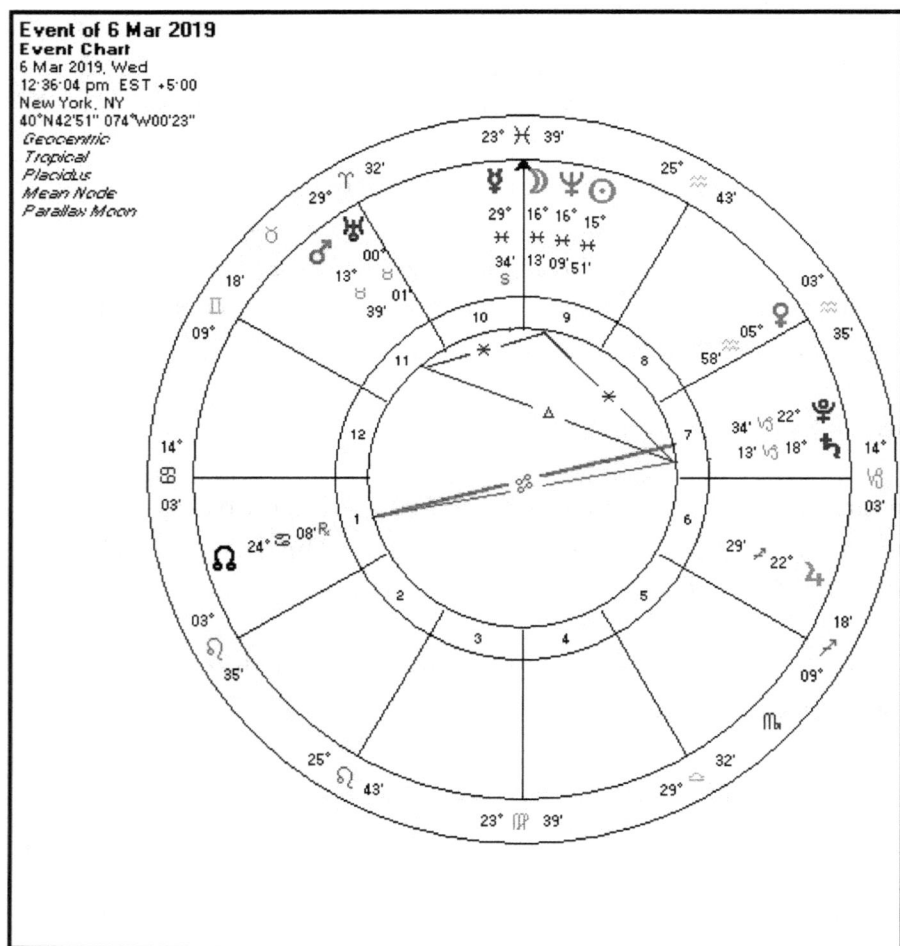

Event of 6 Mar 2019
Event Chart
6 Mar 2019, Wed
12:36:04 pm EST +5:00
New York, NY
40°N42'51" 074°W00'23"
Geocentric
Tropical
Placidus
Mean Node
Parallax Moon

Figure 45 New Moon March 6, 2019

The lunar cycle commencing at this New Moon will run until April 5, 2019. This is an interesting lunation as it is positioned right at NYSE co-ruler Neptune. There is a favorable 60 degree aspect to the other co-ruler Mars. Mercury will be retrograde during this cycle. Expect high drama during this cycle.

Key dates to be alert to during this lunation include:

March 5: Mercury turns retrograde. Expect the unexpected.

March 7: Moon passes natal mid-Heaven point of 24 Pisces.

March 7: ECB Committee meets to discuss Euro-zone interest rates.

March 11: Moon passes NYSE co-ruler location Mars.

March 14-15: Moon at maximum declination as it passes the key 14 of Cancer location. Moon is 90 degrees Neptune.

March 18-19: Moon passes 90 degrees to Mars and 180 degrees to Neptune as the FED meets to discuss monetary policy.

March 24: Moon passes 180 degrees Mars and 120 degrees Neptune.

March 26: Moon passes 90 degrees Neptune.

March 27: Mercury retrograde complete.

March 28: Moon at minimum declination.

April 1: Moon passes 90 degrees Mars.

April 2019

Key Dates

The New Moon cycle for April 2019 commences on the 5th of April with Sun at 15 degrees Aries. The horoscope in Figure 46 depicts planetary placements just hours after the New Moon as the Ascendant passes 14 Cancer.

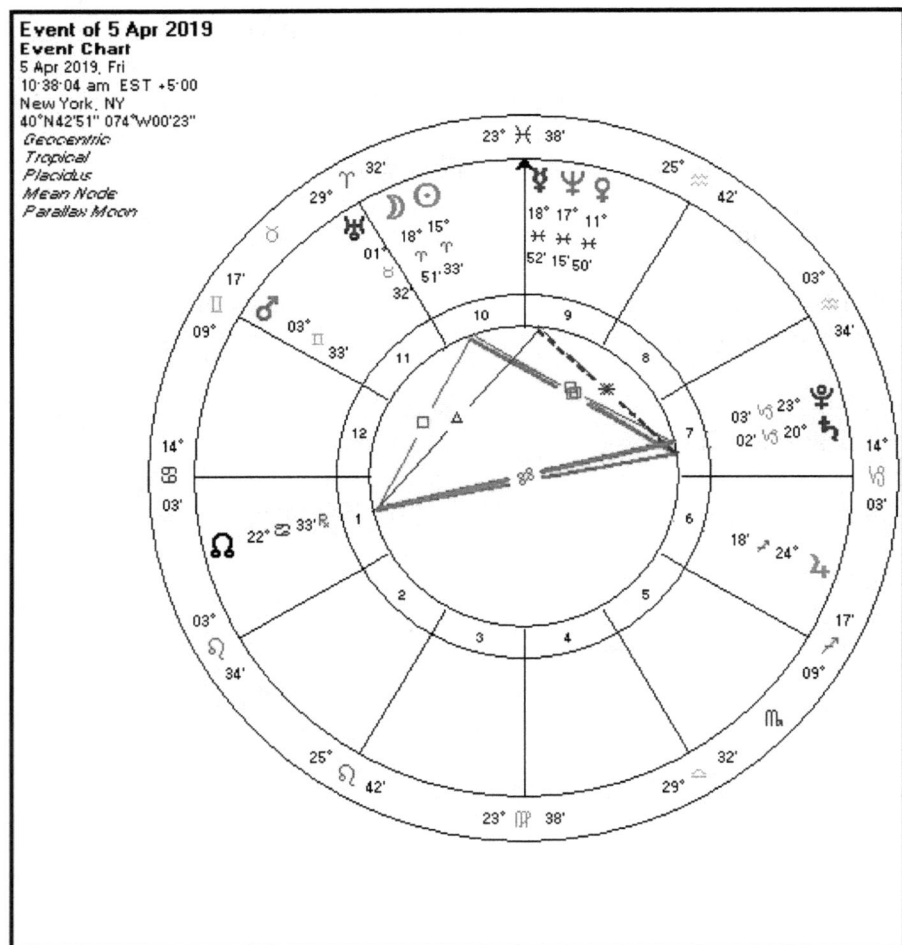

Figure 46 New Moon April 5, 2019

This lunation event is in the most powerful 10th House at the apex of a T-square and 90 degrees square heavy-weight Saturn and within orb of being 90 degrees square the Node. This is suggestive of volatility. However, the lunation is 30 degrees to Neptune which will soften the blow slightly.

Key dates to be alert to during this lunation include:

April 10-12: Moon is at maximum declination. Mercury is at greatest western elongation. Moon passes 90 degrees to Neptune and 120 degrees to Neptune. Expect a trend change of some sort. The ECB meets to discuss Euro zone monetary policy.

April 15- 16: Moon passes 180 degrees to Neptune and 90 degrees to Mars.

April 20-22: This span will see Moon pass 120 degrees to Neptune, 120 degrees to Mars, 180 degrees to Mars and 120 degrees to Neptune.

April 24: Moon at minimum declination.

April 30: Moon passes NYSE co-ruler Neptune and 90 degrees to Mars as the FED meets.

May 1: Moon passes NYSE natal mid-Heaven point of 24 Pisces. There could well be a trend change here of some sort. Watch carefully.

.

May 2019

Key Dates

The New Moon cycle for May 2019 commences on the 4th of May with Sun at 13 degrees Taurus. The horoscope in Figure 47 depicts planetary placements just hours before the New Moon as the Ascendant passes 14 Cancer.

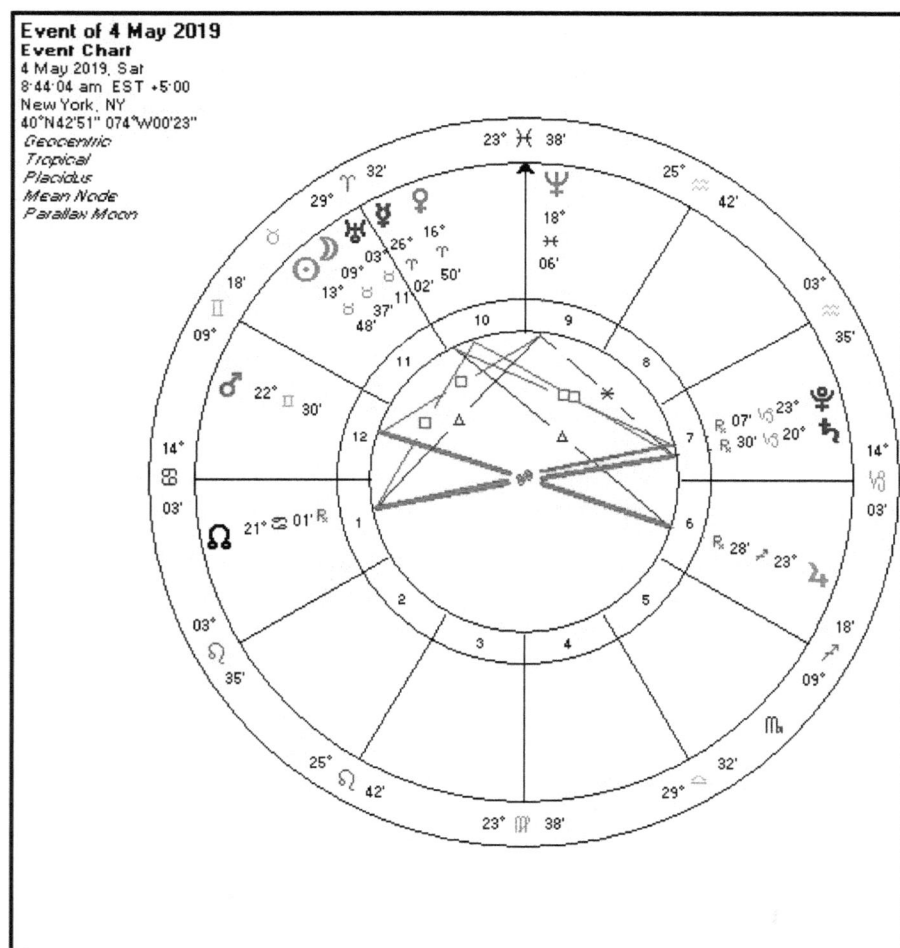

Figure 47 New Moon May 4, 2019

This lunation has no aspects to other planets, save for the approximate 60 degree aspect to Neptune. Mercury and Venus are in the 10th House, with Venus at the apex of a T-square formation involving Node and Saturn. Pluto and Saturn take up residence in the 7th. However, the two co-ruling planets (Mars and Neptune) are at a 90 degree aspect to one another, with Neptune in orb to the mid-Heaven. This could add momentum to the events of April 30-May 1. Look for powerful energies to be released this cycle.

Key dates to be alert to during this lunation include:

May 7: Moon passes NYE co-ruler Mars as it squares (90 degree) Neptune.

May 9: Moon at maximum declination as it makes a 120 degrees aspect to Neptune.

May 9: Moon passes the 14 of Cancer point.

May 14-16: Moon passes 90 degrees to Mars and 120 degrees to Mars

May 17: Moon passes 180 degrees Neptune.

May 20-21: Venus reaches maximum declination and Moon passes square Neptune and opposite Mars.

May 22: Moon at minimum declination.

May 26-27: Moon passes NYSE co-ruler Neptune and is trine Mars.

May 28-29: Moon passes natal mid-Heaven point of 24 Pisces and is square Mars.

.

June 2019

Key Dates

The New Moon for June 2019 commences on the 3rd of June with Sun at 12 degrees Gemini. The horoscope in Figure 48 depicts planetary placements just hours after the New Moon as the Ascendant passes 14 Cancer.

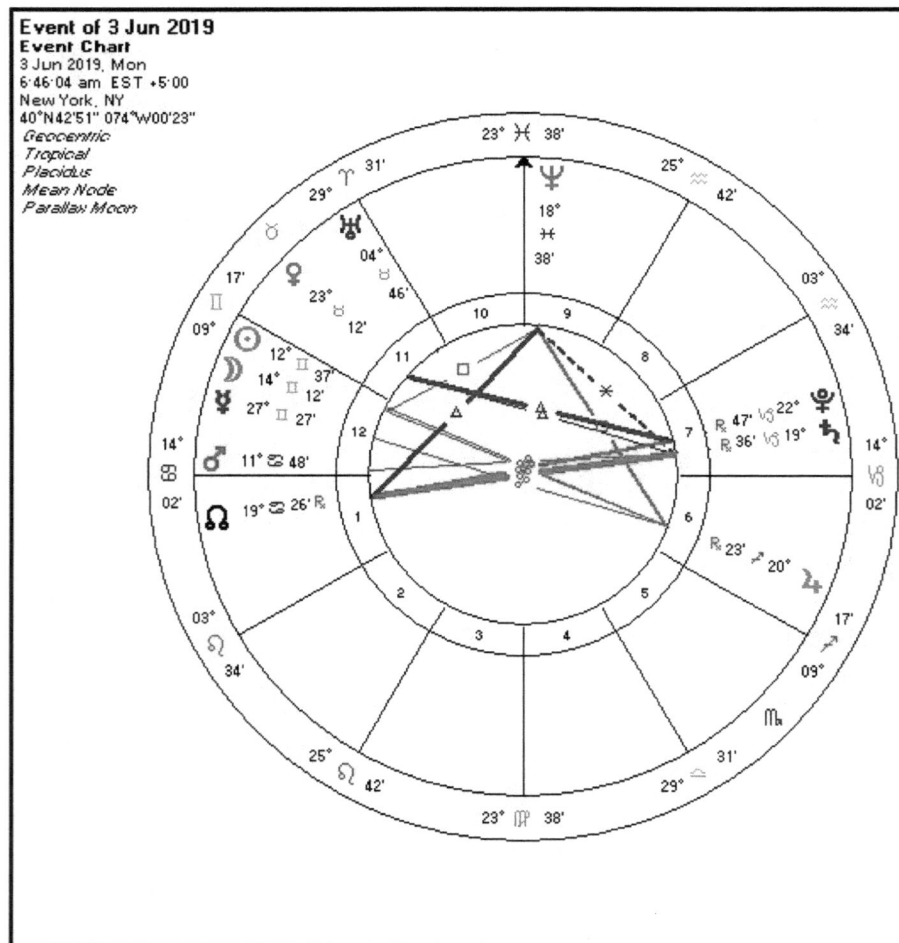

Figure 48 New Moon June 3, 2019

This lunation has no planets in the 10th House. has some potent aspects to it. Mars, the NYE co-ruler, sits practically atop the critical 14 of Cancer point. The New Moon is within orb of a hard 90 degree aspect to the other NYSE co-ruler Neptune which is within orb of being at the NYSE natal mid-Heaven point of 24 Pisces. Expect some gripping drama in this cycle. Key dates to be alert to during this lunation include:

June 5: Moon at maximum declination.

June 5: Moon passes NYSE co-ruler Mars and also the 14 of Cancer point. Moon passes trine Neptune (120 degrees). The ECB meets to review Euro zone monetary policy.

June 9-11: Moon passes opposite Neptune and square Mars.

June 14-16: Moon passes trine Neptune, trine Mars and square Neptune.

June 19: Moon at minimum declination, passing 180 degrees Mars. This span from June 14 to June 19 could deliver a trend change. The FED announces interest rate decision.

June 23: Mercury at greatest eastern elongation. Moon trine Mars.

June 24: Moon passes NYSE co-ruler Neptune and the 24 of Pisces point.

June 27: Moon passes square Mars.

July 2019

Key Dates

The New Moon cycle for July commences on July 2 with Sun at 10 degrees Cancer. The horoscope in Figure 49 depicts planetary placements several hours prior to the New Moon as the Ascendant passes 14 Cancer.

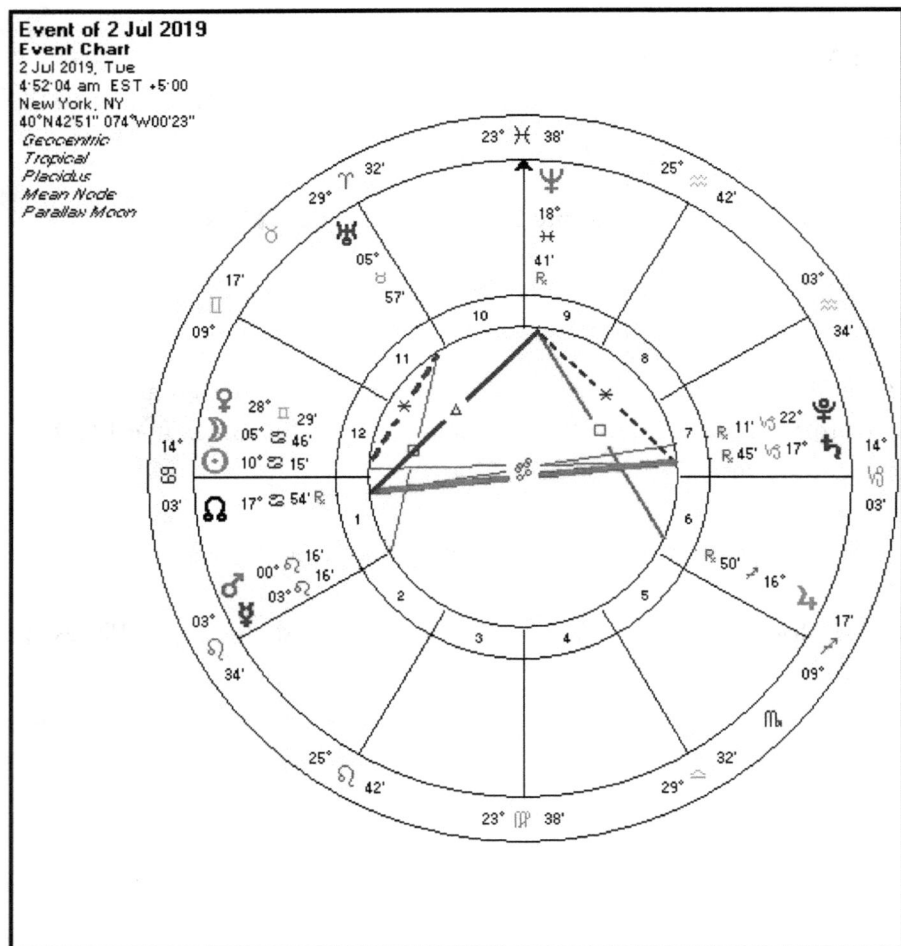

Figure 49 New Moon July 2, 2019

The lunar cycle commencing at this New Moon will run until August 1, 2019. This lunation is unique in that it is within orb of being atop the 14 of Cancer point. This is akin to sitting on top of a keg of dynamite. Will the fuse get lit in this cycle? There are no other visible aspects of this lunation to any other planets, save for a wide orb that arguably places the lunation 180 degrees opposite Saturn. This is potentially good news. However, traders and investors should note that Mercury will be retrograde July 7 to July 31. A trend change is highly possible as retrograde unfolds.

Key dates to be alert to during this lunation include:

July 3: Moon at maximum declination. Moon trine Neptune.

July 4: Moon passes NYSE co-ruler Mars. Markets in New York will be closed this day, so watch for a reaction on July 3.

July 7: Mercury turns retrograde. Expect the unexpected. Moon passes opposite Neptune.

July 10-11: Moon passes square Mars and trine Neptune.

July 15: Moon at minimum declination and square Neptune.

July 22-23: Moon passes co-ruler Neptune and the 24 Pisces natal mid-Heaven point. Moon passes trine Mars.

July 25: The ECB Committee meets to discuss Euro zone monetary policy.

July 26-28: Moon passes square Mars and square Neptune.

July 30: Moon passes the 14 of Cancer point as it also passes minimum declination and trine Neptune. The FED meets to decide on interest rates.

August 2019

Key Dates

The New Moon cycle for August commences on August 2 with Sun at 8 degrees Leo. The horoscope in Figure 50 depicts planetary placements mere hours after the New Moon as the Ascendant passes 14 Cancer. The lunar cycle commencing at this New Moon will run until August 30, 2019.

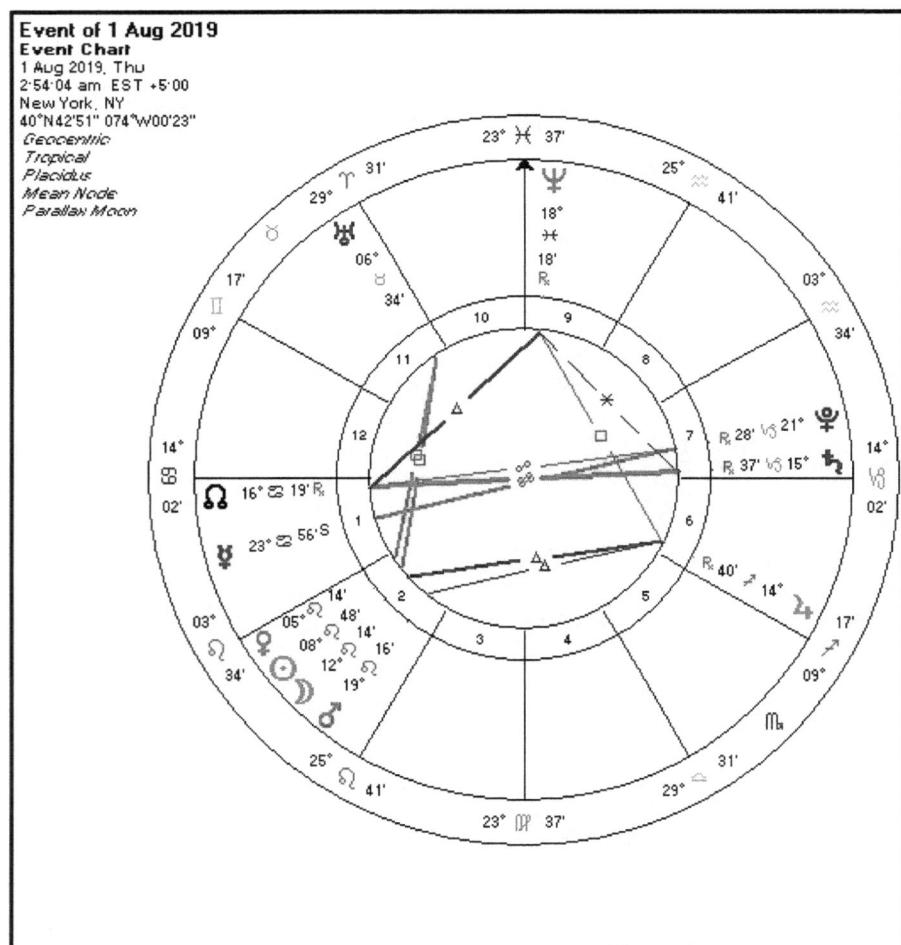

Figure 50 New Moon August 1, 2019

This lunation is trine to expansive planet Jupiter and this lunation follows tight on the heels of Mercury retrograde ending. There are no other aspects to any planets. It is interesting to note that this lunation in Leo has the Sun exalted as Sun is the ruler of the sign of Leo. There could well be a trend change in the early part of this cycle (if it has not already occurred with Mercury retrograde in the previous cycle). This stands to be a decent cycle, barring any unforeseen and bizarre geo-political events coming from the White House in Washington.

Key dates to be alert to during this lunation include:

August 2: Moon passes NYSE co-ruler Mars and opposite Neptune.

August 7-10: Mercury at maximum westerly elongation. Moon passes trine Neptune, square Mars, square Neptune and trine Mars. This span of time will deliver any trend change.

August 12: Moon at maximum declination.

August 16: Moon opposite Mars.

August 17: Sun passes co-ruler Neptune and also the 24 Pisces point. This is a week-end, so watch for a reaction either on the Friday before or the Monday after.

August 21-23: Moon at minimum declination and passes trine Mars, square Mars and square Neptune. Look for another perhaps minor trend change.

August 27: Moon passes the 14 of Cancer point as it makes maximum declination and passes trine Neptune.

September 2019

Key Dates

The New Moon for the September lunar cycle occurs August 30 with Sun at 6 degrees Virgo. The horoscope in Figure 51 depicts planetary placements at the New Moon as the Ascendant passes 14 Cancer.

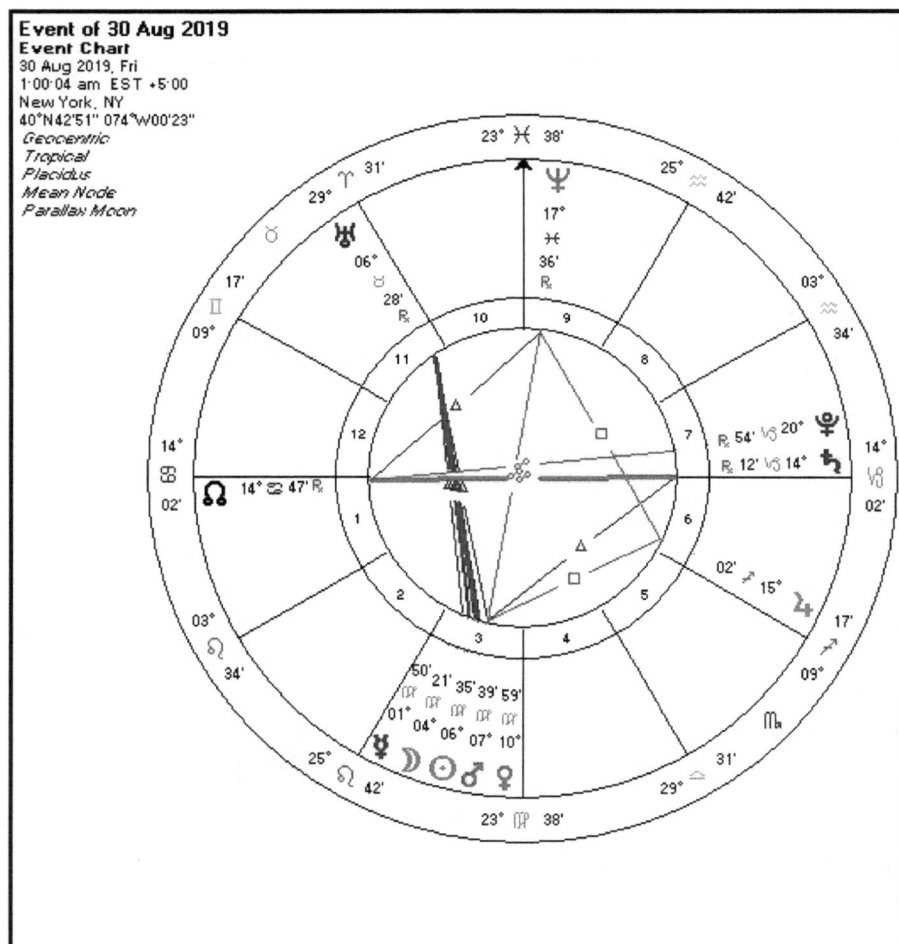

Event of 30 Aug 2019
Event Chart
30 Aug 2019, Fri
1:00:04 am EST +5:00
New York, NY
40°N42'51" 074°W00'23"
Geocentric
Tropical
Placidus
Mean Node
Parallax Moon

Figure 51 New Moon August 30, 2019

The lunar cycle commencing at this New Moon will run until September 28, 2019. This is a peculiar lunation with it being positioned atop NYSE co-ruler Mars and with Mars and the New Moon being 120 degrees to heavy-weight change-maker Uranus. Node sits atop the 14 of Cancer point, held in check by Saturn 180 degrees opposite. This portends an energized cycle on the market. Stay focused.

Key dates to be alert to during this lunation include:

August 30: Moon passes NYSE co-ruler Mars.

September 4: Moon passes trine Neptune.

September 6-8: Moon passes square both Mars and Neptune. Moon at minimum declination. Moon then passes trine Mars.

September 12: The FED meets to decide on interest rates.

September 13-14: Moon passes opposite Mars and then passes co-ruler Neptune and 24 Pisces point. This is a week-end , so watch for a reaction on the Friday before or the Monday after.

September 17-18: The ECB Committee meets to discuss interest rates.

September 19: Moon passes trine Mars.

September 21-23: Moon passes square Mars and Neptune. Moon at maximum declination.

September 23: Moon passes the 14 of Cancer point.

September 27: Moon passes opposite Neptune.

October 2019

Key Dates

The New Moon for the October lunar cycle occurs September 28 with Sun at 5 degrees Libra. The horoscope in Figure 52 depicts planetary placements at the New Moon hours before the Ascendant passes 14 Cancer.

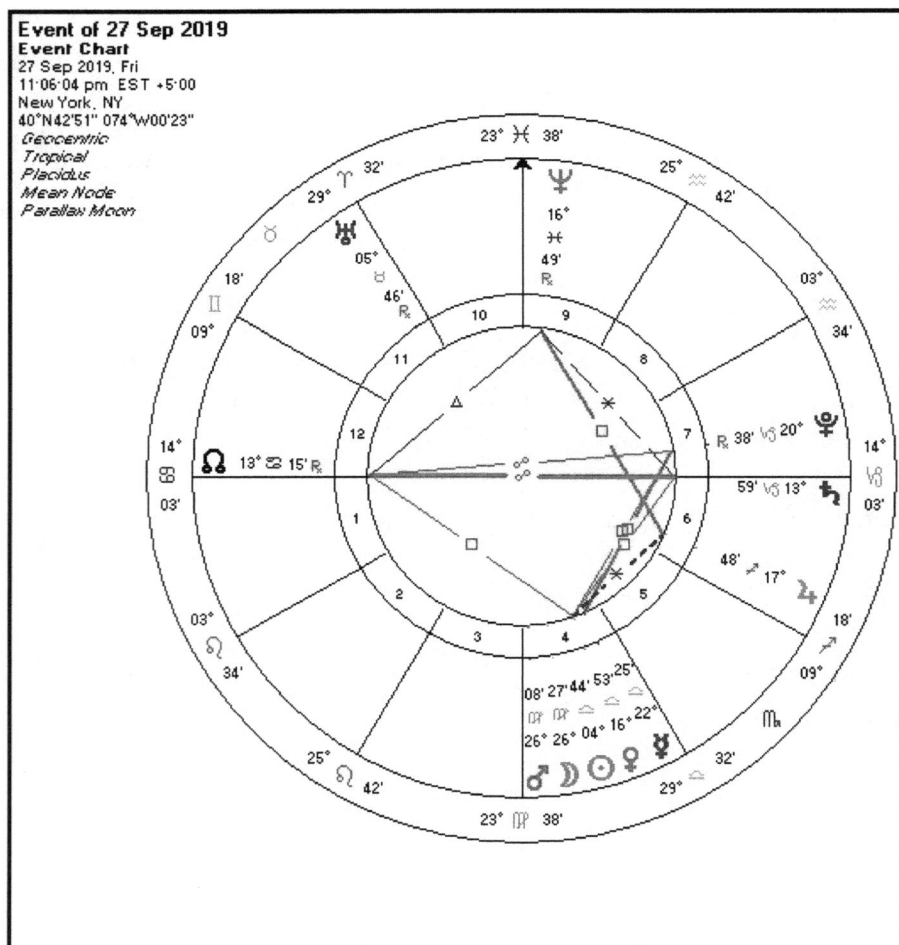

Figure 52 New Moon September 27, 2019

The lunar cycle commencing at this New Moon will run until October 28, 2018. Mars is within orb of being conjunct the lunation, so expect heightened drama with aggressive Mars in the driver's seat.

Key dates to be alert to during this lunation include:

October 1: Moon passes trine Neptune.

October 3-4: Moon passes square Neptune and Mars.

October 5-7: Moon at minimum declination and trine Mars.

October 10-12: Moon passes co-ruler Neptune, Moon passes 24 of Pisces point and opposite Mars.

October 17-18: Moon passes trine Mars and square Neptune.

October 19: Moon passes the 14 of cancer point. This is a week-end, so watch for a reaction on the Friday before.

October 20: Mercury is at its greatest easterly elongation and Moon passes square Mars and trine Neptune. Watch for a small trend change, as Moon is also at maximum declination.

October 24: The ECB Committee meets to review interest rates in the Euro-zone.

October 26: Moon passes co-ruler Mars. This is a week-end, so watch for a reaction on the Friday before.

November 2019

Key Dates

The New Moon for the November lunar cycle occurs on the 27th of October with Sun at 4 degrees Scorpio. The horoscope in Figure 53 depicts planetary placements several hours prior to the New Moon as the Ascendant passes 14 Cancer.

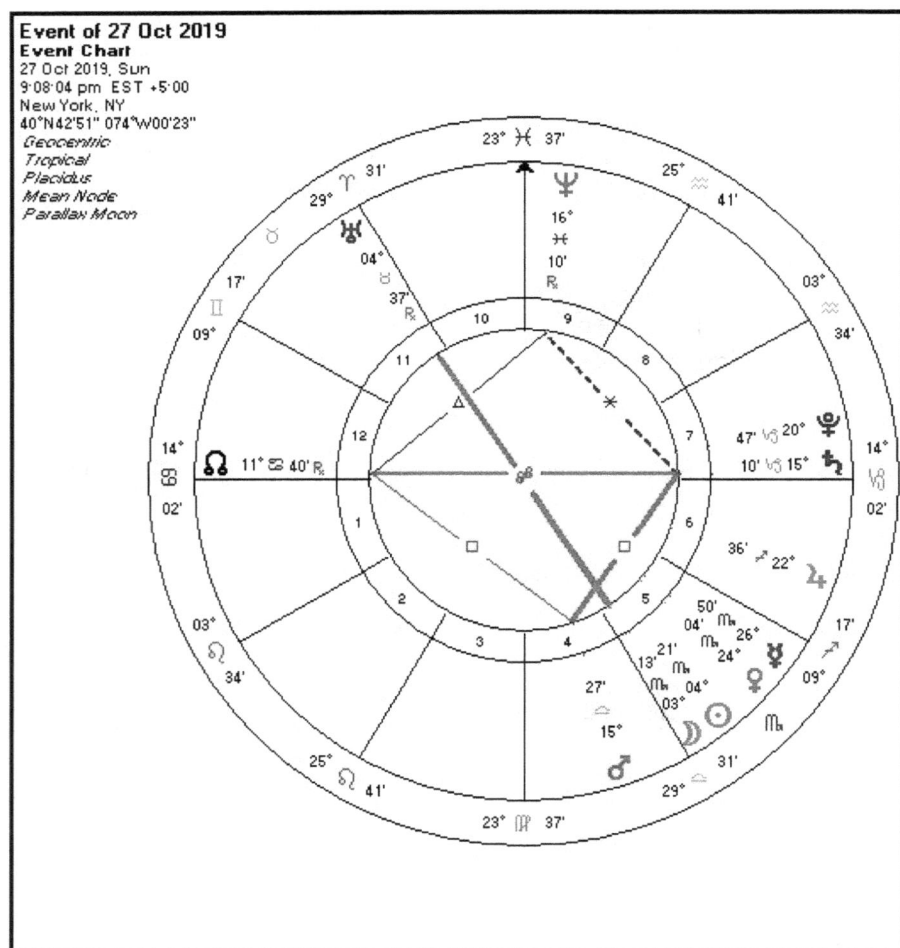

Figure 53 New Moon October 27, 2019

This lunation is 180 degrees opposite heavy-weight Uranus and there are no planets in the 10th House. However, Mercury turns retrograde on October 31 and remains so until November 19. With little else to keep Mercury in check during this retrograde, expect the unexpected.

Key dates to be alert to during this lunation include:

October 29-30: The FED meets to decide on interest rates.

October 31: Mercury turns retrograde. Expect the unexpected.

November 1-2: Moon square Mars. Moon at minimum declination. A trend change is likely.

November 5: Moon trine Mars.

November 7: Moon passes co-ruler Neptune and the 24 of Pisces point.

November 14-17: Moon passes square Neptune, trine Mars, Moon at maximum declination. Moon passes the 14 of Cancer point. This is a Saturday, so expect a market reaction on the Friday before. A trend change of sorts could occur. Moon passes square Mars. Mercury retrograde wrapping up.

November 21-23: Moon passes opposite Neptune. Moon passes co-ruler Mars. This is a Saturday, so expect a market reaction on the Friday before.

November 25: Moon passes trine Neptune.

.

December 2019

Key Dates

The New Moon for the December lunar cycle occurs on November 26 with Sun at 4 Sagittarius. The horoscope in Figure 54 depicts planetary placements several hours after the New Moon as the Ascendant passes 14 Cancer.

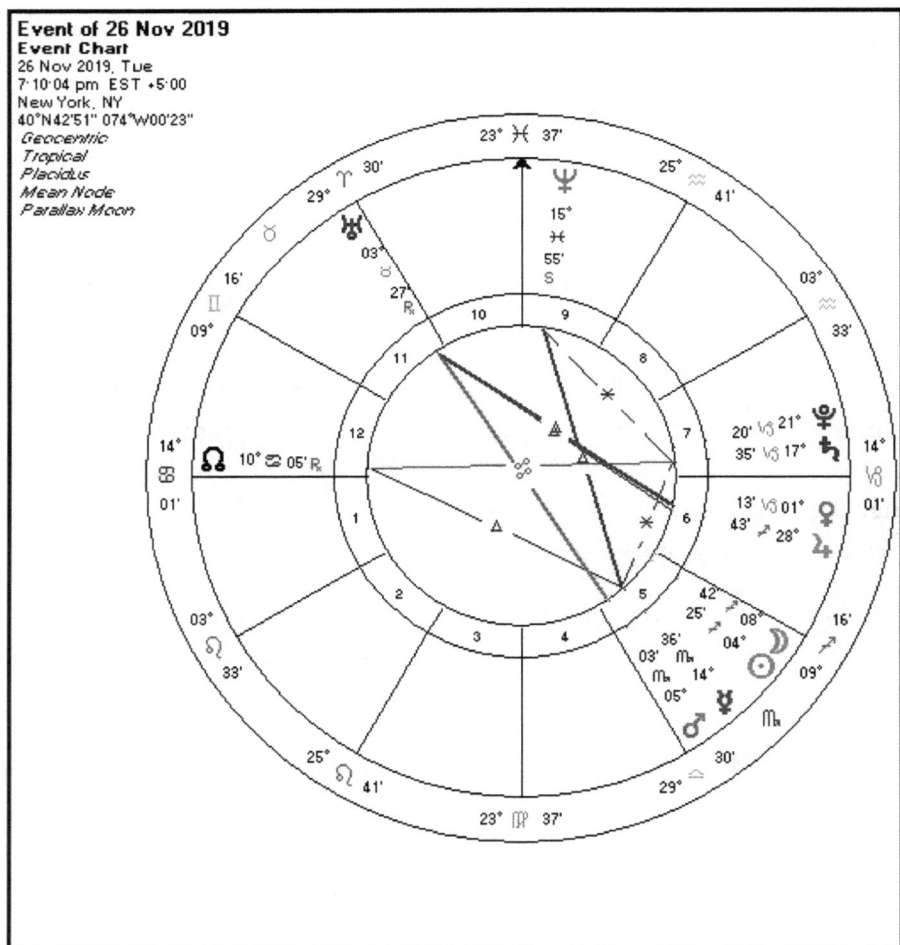

Figure 54 New Moon November 26, 2019

The lunar cycle commencing at this New Moon will run until December 26, 2019. The only aspect to the lunation is a soft 30 degrees to Mars. This cycle should be generally favorable.

Key dates to be alert to during this lunation include:

November 28: Mercury at greatest westerly elongation.

November 30: Moon at minimum declination. This early part of the cycle could see a trend change of some sort.

December 1-4: Moon passes square Mars, trine Mars and Moon passes co-ruler Neptune and the 24 Pisces point.

December 11-14: Moon passes square Neptune. Moon at maximum declination as it passes the 14 of Cancer point. Moon passes trine to both Mars and Neptune. The FED and ECB are both meeting to decide on interest rates.

December 22: Moon passes co-ruler Mars. This is a Sunday, so watch for a market reaction on the next day-Monday. Sun is approaching a 0 degree aspect to Jupiter. Such aspects have a high propensity for trend changes. Moon also passes trine Neptune.

December 26: New Moon and a new trading year will get underway.

Albano – An Alternative Interpretation

This look at the NYSE for 2019 through the eyes of Loiuse McWhirter begs the question – are there any other techniques for examining the markets? In fact there is and it comes from an obscure Italian philosophical mind called Giacomo Albano.

Albano's work centers around the *'Syzygy'*. By definition, a Syzygy is a pairing of planets or bodies. Albano uses Sun-Moon pairings of New Moons and Full Moons in his work. Also, he focuses on the New Moon or the Full Moon that occurs immediately prior to Sun transiting into a Cardinal Sign. Cardinal Signs are Aries, Cancer, Libra and Capricorn. We all have plenty of experience with Cardinal Signs. Sun moving into Aries is our Spring Equinox. Sun moving into Cancer marks the Summer Solstice just as Sun moving into Libra marks the Autumn Equinox. Sun moving into Capricorn marks the Winter Solstice which we regard as the start of Winter. As for location, Albano structures his horoscope wheels for Greenwich, England.

The Financial Houses

Albano clearly states that the 2nd, 5th and 8th Houses of the zodiac wheel are those that pertain to the markets. Each of these Houses is "ruled" by a certain planet. The "ruler" is determined by the zodiac sign that the House is in. These ruler-ships go way back in history. The data in Figure 55 presents the zodiac signs and their rulers. You will recognize at least a portion of this data. Recall from the McWhirter analysis that the NYSE natal mid-Heaven straddled Pisces and Aries. McWhirter stated that Mars and Neptune ruled the NYSE. Figure 55 shows that indeed these planets do rule Pisces and Aries.

Zodiac Sign	Ruling Planet
Aries	Mars
Taurus	Venus
Gemini	Mercury
Cancer	Moon
Leo	Sun
Virgo	Mercury
Libra	Venus
Scorpio	Mars and Pluto
Sagittarius	Jupiter
Capricorn	Saturn
Aquarius	Saturn and Uranus
Pisces	Neptune and Jupiter

Figure 55 Houses and Rulers

For example, if a House division starts in the sign of Aries, Albano says that Mars rules that House because Mars is the "ruler" of Aries. Albano then goes on to consider whether the 2nd, 5th or 8th Houses contain any planets that are in *'exaltation'* or *'exile'*. Both of these notions are rooted deep in classical Astrology. He then determines what planet is the *'dominus'* of the horoscope wheel. That is, what planet (if any) is conjunct the New Moon occurrence. He further looks to see what planets are *'in their terms'*, which I take to mean 'happy'. What emerges from this review of a horoscope wheel is a listing of *FS planets*, where (FS) denotes Financially Significant.

Patterns

Once Albano has assessed the planets in the 2nd, 5th and 8th Houses (and the rulers of those Houses), he looks to see if these FS bodies form a discernable geometric pattern. Classical Astrology assigns positive and negative energies to various geometric patterns. If the pattern has positive connotations, Albano then says the markets will generally do well from the Syzygy being analyzed through until the next similar Syzygy. A negative pattern portends a less than favorable outcome. He regards the *Point of Thales* pattern as positive. *Kites* and *Grand Trines* are also highly regarded. *Grand Crosses* and *T-Squares* are signs of negative energy. *Yods* are tending towards the negative.

A T-Square is a right angled triangle with two equal sides.

A Grand Cross is two T-Squares put together to form a big square pattern.

A Grand Trine is an equilateral triangle where all angles are 120 degrees.

A Point of Thales is a right-angled triangle where the three planets in question are at 120 degrees, 180 degrees and 60 degrees from each other.

A Yod is a formation involving three planets where angular separations are 150, 150 and 60 degrees.

The data in Figure 56 shows what bodies are exalted and exiled where.

Zodiac Sign	Exaltation	Exile
Aries	Sun 18-19 degrees Aries	Saturn
Taurus	Moon 2-3 degrees Taurus	
Gemini		
Cancer	Jupiter 14-15 degrees Cancer	Mars
Leo		
Virgo	Mercury 14-15 degrees Virgo	Venus
Libra	Saturn 20-21 degrees Libra	Sun
Scorpio		Moon
Sagittarius		
Capricorn	Mars 27-28 degrees Capricorn	Jupiter
Aquarius		
Pisces	Venus 26-27 degrees Pisces	Mercury

Figure 56 Exaltation and Exile

The data in Figure 57 shows the degree ranges where planets are in their terms.

Aries	Jupiter 0-6	Venus 6-14	Mercury 14-21	Mars 21-26	Saturn 26-20
Taurus	Venus 0-8	Mercury 8-15	Jupiter 15-22	Saturn 22-26	Mars 26-20
Gemini	Mercury 0-7	Jupiter 7-14	Venus 14-21	Saturn 21-25	Mars 25-30
Cancer	Mars 0-6	Jupiter 6-13	Mercury 13-20	Venus 20-27	Saturn 27-30
Leo	Saturn 0-6	Mercury 6-13	Venus 13-19	Jupiter 19-25	Mars 25-30
Virgo	Mercury 0-6	Venus 7-13	Jupiter 13-18	Saturn 18-24	Mars 24-30
Libra	Saturn 0-6	Venus 6-11	Jupiter 11-19	Mercury 19-24	Mars 24-30
Scorpio	Mars 0-6	Jupiter 6-14	Venus 14-21	Mercury 21-27	Saturn 27-30
Sagittarius	Jupiter 0-8	Venus 8-14	Mercury 14-19	Saturn 19-25	Mars 25-30
Capricorn	Venus 0-6	Mercury 6-12	Jupiter 12-19	Mars 19-25	Saturn 25-30
Aquarius	Saturn 0-6	Mercury 6-12	Venus 12-20	Jupiter 20-25	Mars 25-30
Pisces	Venus 0-8	Jupiter 8-14	Mercury 14-20	Mars 20-26	Saturn 26-30

Figure 57 Terms

What follows now is a re-examination of the NYSE for 2019 from Syzygy to Syzygy, where I take a Syzygy to be a New Moon event. I am not going to re-show all of the horoscope wheels with the New Moon events. Rather, I am going to simply summarize what the Albano method tells me.

New Moon of January 6, 2019: There are no planets in the 2nd House, ruled by Venus. The 5th House (ruled by Saturn) contains Pluto within orb of being conjunct the lunation. The 8th House (ruled by Mars) contains Uranus. There are no exaltations. Financially significant planets in this horoscope are thus Venus, Saturn, Mars and Uranus and Pluto. The only aspect among these is a trine between Venus and Mars. Expect heavy-weight Pluto to weigh forcfully on matters.

New Moon of February 4, 2019: There are no planets in the 2nd House which is ruled by Mars and Pluto. Venus, Saturn and Pluto appear in the 5th House which is in Sagittarius ruled by Jupiter. There are no planets in the 8th House ruled by Neptune and Jupiter. Mercury is within orb of being conjunct the Sun and so is the dominus. No planets are in exaltation. The only pattern apparent is a T-square with one apex at Pluto. This syzygy is suggestive of a lunar cycle weighed back and kept in check by the 90 degree aspects between Mars and Saturn and Neptune and Jupiter.

New Moon of March 6, 2019: There are no planets in the 2nd House or the 5th House. The 8th House contains Saturn, Pluto and Venus. NYSE co-ruler Neptune is atop the lunation and is therefore the dominus. Saturn is at home in Capricorn where it rules. Saturn is a 60 degree angle to Neptune. The (FS) planets are thus Venus, Saturn and Neptune. With Mercury turning retrograde in this lunar cycle, look for some drama.

New Moon of April 5, 2019: The 2nd House is in Aries, ruled by Mars contains the lunation. The 5th House, ruled by Mercury, contains no planets. The 8th House, ruled by Venus, contains no planets. There is a curiously interesting Point of Thales pattern evident in the horoscope involving Saturn, Node and Mercury at the apex. No planets are in exaltation or exile or terms. A Point of Thales pattern is regarded by Albano as positive. Therefore, this syzygy infers more positive market behaviour than the month prior.

New Moon of May 4, 2019: The 2nd House is in Sagittarius and is ruled by Jupiter. The 2nd House contains Jupiter, Saturn and Pluto, so Jupiter is at home. The 5th House is in Aries, ruled by Mars, and contains Venus and Mercury. The 8th House is in Gemini, ruled by Mercury, and contains Mars. There is a T-square pattern evident involving Saturn and Mars with Venus at its apex. There is also a Point of Thales pattern with Saturn at one of the corners. Lots of energy at work here.

New Moon of June 3, 2019: The 2nd House is in Gemini, ruled by Mercury, and contains Mars. The 5th House is in Virgo, ruled by Mercury, and contains no planets. The 8th House is in Sagittarius, ruled by Jupiter, and contains no planets. Mercury, Mars and Jupiter are this FS planets, but Jupiter is retrograde and therefore slightly impaired. There are no chart patterns evident in this horoscope. This analysis suggests to watch for Mars to exert its energies.

New Moon of July 2, 2019: The 2nd House is in Sagittarius ruled by Jupiter and contains Jupiter. Expansive Jupiter is thus at home. The 5th House is in Pisces, ruled by Neptune and Jupiter, and contains no planets. The 8th House is in Gemini, ruled by Mercury, and contains Venus and the lunation. There are no patterns, no exaltations and no terms. The only aspect I see between two FS planets is a 90 degree aspect between Neptune and Jupiter. Expect volatility as expansive Jupiter is influenced by Neptune.

New Moon of August 1, 2019: The 2nd House is in Gemini, ruled by Mercury, and contains no planets. The 5th House is in Leo, ruled by Sun, and contains the lunation. Sun is therefore at home. The 8th House is in Sagittarius, ruled by Jupiter, and contains Jupiter. Jupiter and Sun are thus FS. I see no chart patterns aside from a trine between Jupiter and the lunation. This lunar cycle will therefore offer up some drama.

New Moon of August 30, 2019: The 2nd House is in Virgo, ruled by Mercury, and contains no planets. The 5th House is in Sagittarius, ruled by Jupiter, and contains Saturn and Pluto. The 8th House is in Pisces, ruled by Neptune and Jupiter, and contains Neptune. The lunation itself sits atop Mars, thus making aggressive Mars the dominus. Mercury and Venus are in their terms in Virgo. The (FS) planets are thus Saturn, Pluto, Mars, Venus, Jupiter and Neptune. Mars, Neptune and Jupiter figure prominently in a T-Square pattern. Plenty of energy at work here. Expect high energy. Stay focused.

New Moon of September 28, 2019: The 2nd House is in Aquarius, ruled by Saturn and Uranus, and contains Neptune. The 5th House is in Taurus, ruled by Venus, and contains no planets. The 8th House is in Leo, ruled by Sun, with Mars present. Mars is in its terms in Virgo and Mercury in its terms in Libra. Mars is the closest planet to the lunation, so is the dominus. I see no chart patterns of any significance involving the (FS) planets Mars, Neptune, and Mercury. Watch for Mars energy to carry the day. Stay focused.

New Moon of October 28, 2019: The 2nd House is in Leo, ruled by Sun, and contains no planets. The 5th House is in Scorpio, ruled by Mars and Pluto, with Mercury and Jupiter present. The 8th House is in Aquarius, ruled by Saturn and Uranus, with Neptune present. I see a Point of Thales pattern with Neptune at its apex. With Neptune being a ruling planet of the NYSE, this cycle could be lively.

New Moon of November 26, 2019: The 2nd House is in Aquarius, ruled by Saturn and Jupiter, with Neptune present. The 5th House is in Taurus, ruled by Venus, with no planets present. The 8th House is in Leo, ruled by Sun, with no planets present. Mars and Venus are in their terms in Scorpio and Capricorn respectively. Scorpio is ruled by Mars. I am not seeing any patterns in this chart. Watch for Mars and Neptune to exert influence during the cycle.

11

Astrology of Commodities in 2019

Gold

Investors who own Gold are accustomed to routinely checking the price of Gold by tuning into a television business channel or perhaps obtaining a live quote of Gold futures. What many do not realize is that Gold is a unique entity - for quietly working behind the scenes is an archaic methodology called the London Gold Fix.

The London Gold Fix occurs at 10:30 am and 3:00 pm local time each business day in London. Participants in the daily fixes are: Barclay's, HSBC, Scotia Mocatta (a division of Scotia Bank of Canada) and Societe Generale. These twice daily collaborations (some would say collusions) provide a benchmark price that is then used around the globe to settle and mark-to-market all the various Gold-related derivative contracts in existence.

The history of the Gold Fix is a fascinating one. On the 12th of September 1919, the Bank of England made arrangements with N.M. Rothschild & Sons for the formation of a Gold market in which there would be one official price for Gold quoted on any one day. At 11:00 am, the first Gold fixing took place, with the five principal gold bullion traders and refiners of the day performing the first gold fixing. These traders and refiners were N.M. Rothschild & Sons, Mocatta & Goldsmid, Pixley & Abell, Samuel Montagu & Co. and Sharps Wilkins.

The horoscope in Figure 58 depicts planetary positions at this date in history. Observations that jump off the page include: North Node had just changed signs, Venus was retrograde, Sun and Venus were conjunct, Mercury and Saturn were conjunct, Mars, Neptune and

Jupiter were all conjunct at/near the Mid-Heaven point of the horoscope and Saturn was 180 degrees opposite Uranus.

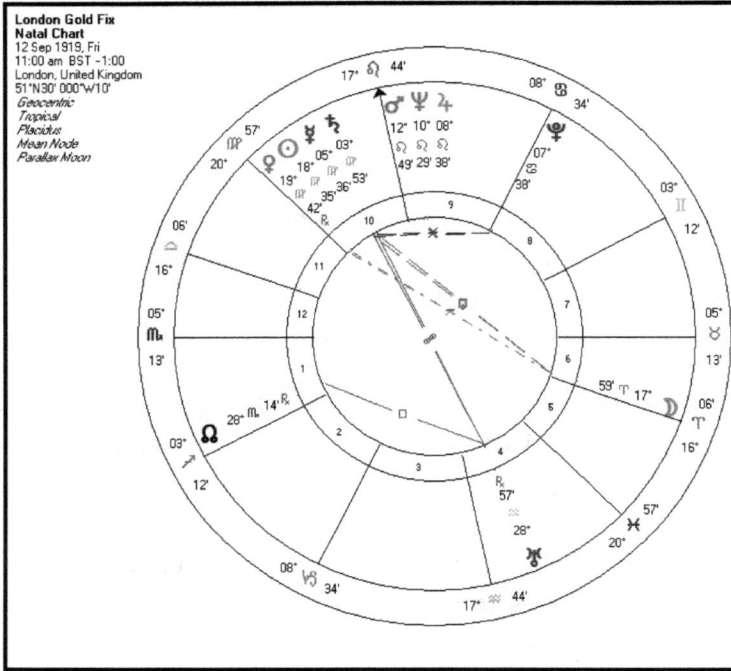

Figure 58 1919 London Gold Fix horoscope

Gold investors who have been around for a while will remember the significant $800/ounce price peak recorded by Gold in January 1980. To illustrate how Astrology is linked to Gold prices consider that at this price peak, the transiting North Node had just changed signs and was 90 degrees hard aspect to the natal Node in the 1919 horoscope. Consider too that Mars and Jupiter were both coming into a 0 degree conjunction with the natal Sun location in the 1919 horoscope. For those who were involved in Gold more recently, recall that Gold hit a significant peak in early September 2011 at just over $1900/ounce. At that peak, Sun and Venus were conjunct to one another as they were in the 1919 Gold Fix horoscope. What's more, they were within a few degrees of being conjunct to the natal Sun location in the 1919 horoscope. A coincidence you say? I say not.

In the few weeks that followed this 2011 peak, Gold prices plunged nearly $400/ounce. But, then Gold found its legs again and began to rally. This rally seems directly related to Mars being 90 degrees hard aspect to Jupiter. In addition, Mars was drawing into a 0 degree conjunction to the Mars-Jupiter-Neptune location of the 1919 horoscope wheel.

Such is the complex nature of Gold prices. I have studied past charts of Gold and I am shocked at how many price inflection points are related in one way or another to the Astrology of the 1919 Gold Fix horoscope wheel. To those readers who are of the opinion that Gold price is manipulated – your notion is indeed a valid one and it is my firm belief that Astrology is the secret language being spoken amongst those that play a hand in the manipulation.

But, traders and investors in Gold do not just rely on the daily London Fix for price indication. There is also the Gold futures market. Gold futures started trading on the New York Mercantile Exchange on December 31, 1974.

Figure 59 illustrates the planetary positions in 1974 at the first trade date of Gold futures. As an interesting exercise, note that in the 1919 chart Mars and Neptune are conjunct one another. Now, observe that Mars and Neptune are also conjunct in the 1974 chart. Next, ask yourself why the New York Mercantile Exchange would launch a new futures contract on December 31 – a time when most staff would be off for Christmas holidays. Take a look at the location of Moon in the 1974 horoscope. Moon is at 11 degrees of Leo. Now, take a look at the 1919 horoscope and observe that 11 degrees of Leo is where Mars and Neptune are located. I take these curious placements as further evidence of an astrological connection between Gold price, the 1919 Gold Fix date and the 1974 first trade date for Gold futures. All very intriguing stuff to be sure.

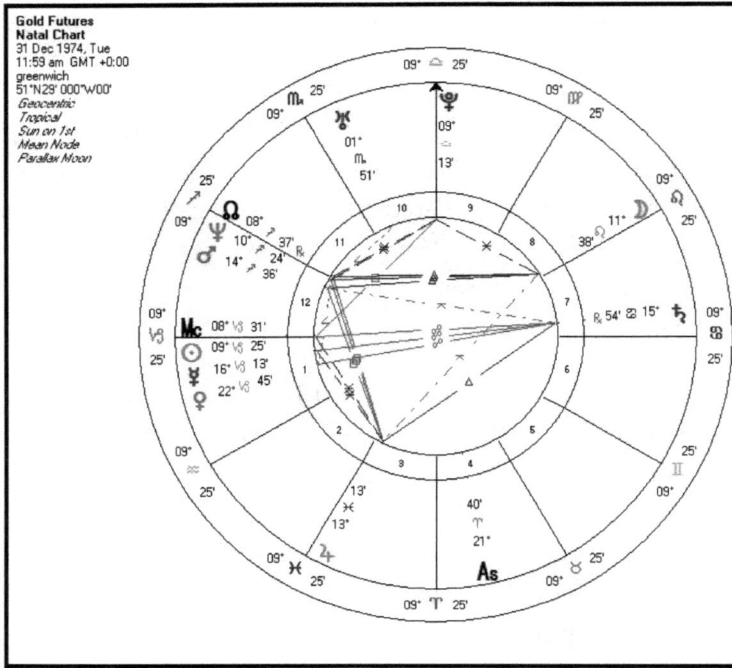

Figure 59 Gold futures First Trade horoscope

Transiting Mars/1974 natal Sun

Transiting Mars passing the natal Sun location from the 1974 First Trade horoscope is a valuable tool for Gold traders to consider. Consider too, the 90 and 180 degree aspects. The chart in Figure 60 has been overlaid with 0, 90 and 180 degree aspects of transiting Mars / natal Sun. Note how these events align to various inflection points on the price chart.

For 2019, transiting Mars will make the following aspects to the 1974 natal Sun location:

January 1– January 28: Mars slowly passes 90 degrees square to natal Sun.

May 16 – June 14: Mars passes 180 degrees to natal Sun.

October 5– October 31: Mars passes 90 degrees to natal Sun

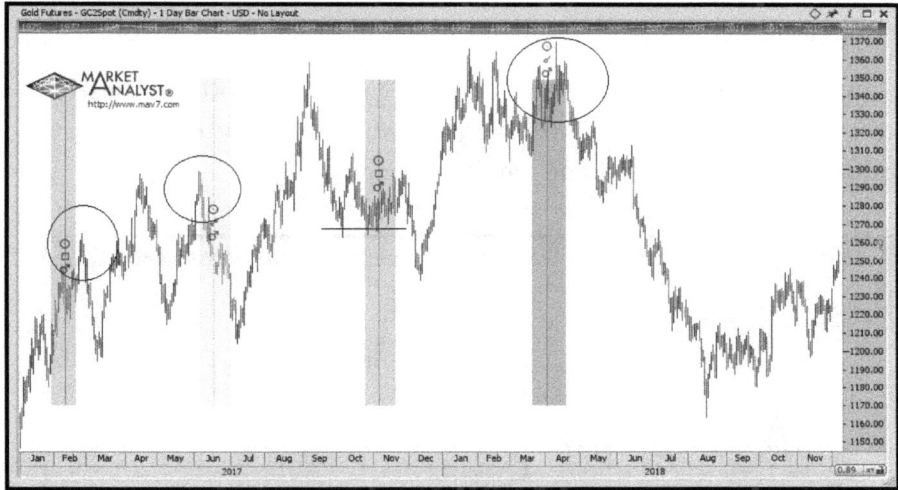

Figure 60 Transiting Mars / natal Sun aspects

Transiting Sun and Mars /1919 natal Sun

As previously noted, aspects to planetary locations in the 1919 Gold Fix horoscope are also important.

For 2019, transiting Sun will make the following aspects to the 1919 natal Sun location:

March 2-March 14: passing 180 degrees opposite to 1919 natal Sun

June 2-June 15: passing 90 degrees to 1919 natal Sun

September 2-September 19:passing 0 degrees conjunct to 1919 natal Sun

December 4-December 16: passing 90 degrees to 1919 natal Sun

For 2019, transiting Mars will make the following aspects to the 1919 natal Sun location:

April 15 - May 11: passing 90 degrees to 1919 natal Sun.

September 3 – September 27: passing 0 degrees conjunct to 1919 natal Sun.

The chart in Figure 61 has been overlaid with 0, 90 and 180 degree aspects of transiting Mars / 1919 natal Sun. Note how these events align to various inflection points on the price chart.

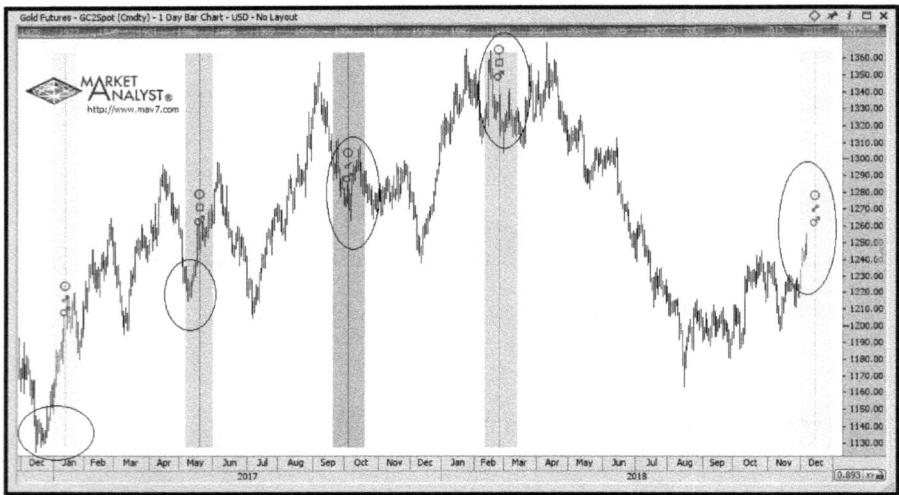

Figure 61 Transiting Mars / 1919 natal Sun aspects

The chart in Figure 62 has been overlaid with 0, 90 and 180 degree aspects of transiting Sun / 1919 natal Sun. Note how these events align to various inflection points on the price chart.

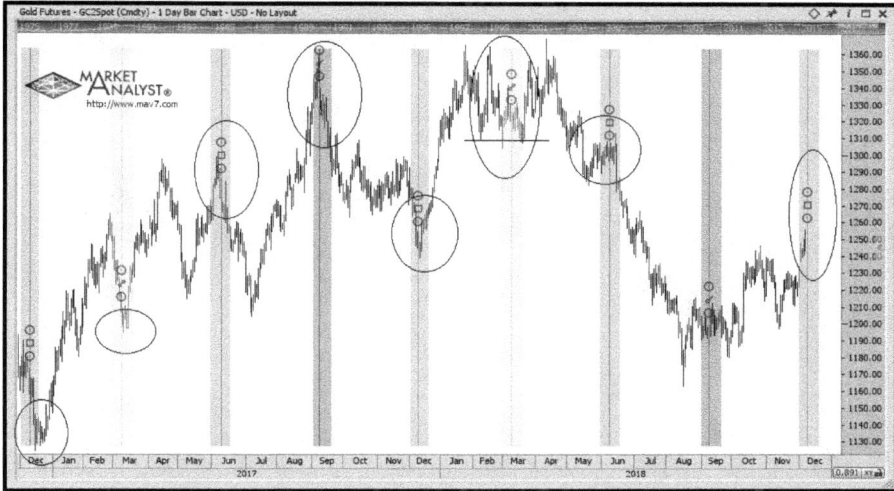

Figure 62 Transiting Sun / 1919 natal Sun aspects

Sun Conjunct Venus

Another cue from the 1919 chart is the conjunction between Sun and Venus. Figure 63 illustrates the effect of Sun/Venus conjunctions on Gold prices. Note the alignment to price inflection points. At the far left of the chart, note that in mid-2016 a Sun/Venus event aligned spot on to a significant low and a subsequent swing high. A similar situation occurred in late 2017. The narrow bands that appear on the chart can best be dis-regarded as these are conjunctions, but with Venus retrograde. In 2019, from July 24 through about September 22, Sun and Venus will be passing in a wide orb of conjunction.

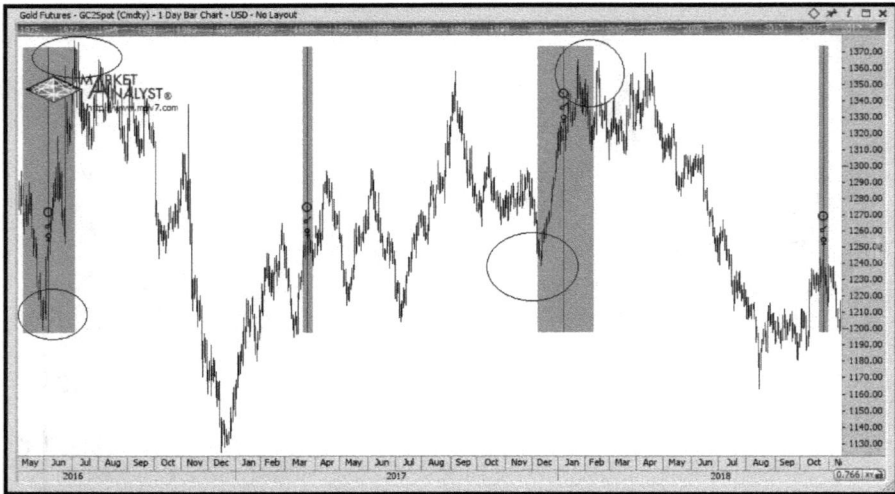

Figure 63 Sun conjunct Venus and Gold prices

Mercury Retrograde

Another valuable tool for Gold traders to consider is Mercury retrograde events. Watch for technical chart trend indictors to suggest a short term trend change at a retrograde event.

The chart in Figure 64 illustrates the connection between these Mercury phenomena and Gold prices. The correlation to swing highs and lows is rather striking.

For 2019, Mercury will be:

➢ In retrograde from March 5 through March 27.

➢ In retrograde from July 7 through July 31.

➢ In retrograde from October 31 through November 19.

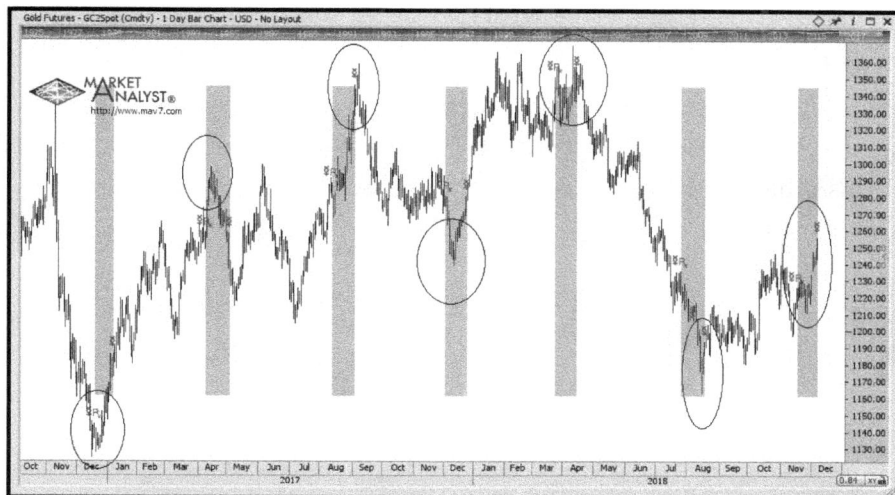

Figure 64 Gold and the Mercury retrograde Influence

Lastly, there is one additional cue to be taken from the 1919 horoscope wheel. Notice that Saturn and Uranus are 180 degrees hard aspect opposite to one another. Times when Saturn and Uranus are 0, 90 or 180 degrees apart should be watched carefully. The last significant price peak on Gold came in September 2011 when these two heavyweight planets were opposite each other.

The good news is, for 2019, there are no such hard aspects between these two planets. There will be a 90 degree square aspect that commences in early 2020 – just in time for the end of the Gann Master Cycle. Amazing how these patterns overlap isn't it?

Reminder - Follow the Trend

The one question that I routinely get from those that follow my writings is – when during one of these astrological transit events should a person implement a trade? The answer is very simple. You should consider implementing a trade when you see the trend change. Always let the trend be your friend. I am sure you have heard this mantra before. I cannot emphasize this mantra enough. There are many ways of measuring trend. My experience has shown me that the methodologies developed by J. Welles Wilder are very powerful for identifying trend changes. In particular I prefer to use his Wilder Volatility Stop. Wilder's 1978 book *New Concepts in Technical Trading Systems* is a highly recommended read if you are seeking to learn more about his methods.

Silver

Silver futures started trading on a recognized financial exchange in July 1933. Figure 65 shows the First Trade horoscope for Silver futures in geocentric format.

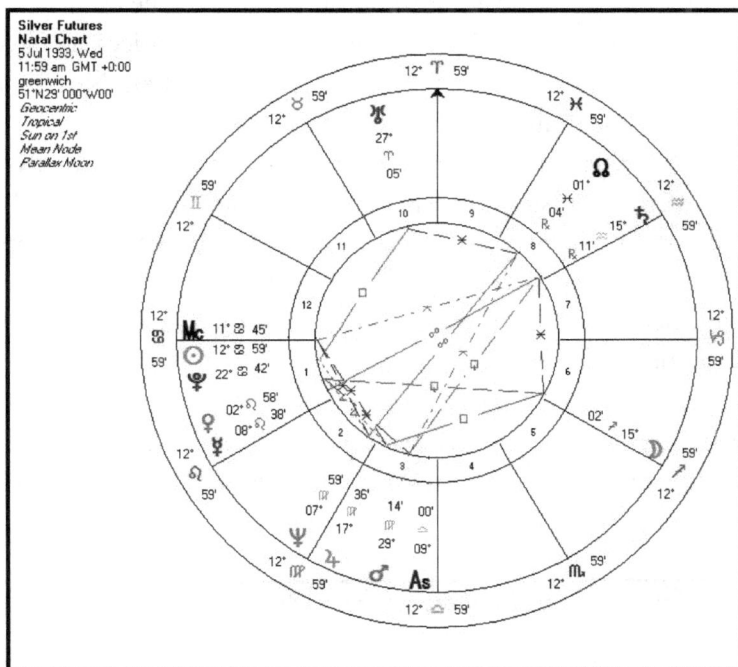

Figure 65 Silver futures First Trade horoscope

My research has shown that times when transiting Sun, transiting Mars and transiting Jupiter make hard aspects to the natal Sun point at 12 degrees Cancer should be watched carefully for evidence of trend changes and price inflection points. I am intrigued with this First Trade date. I suppose Silver could have started trading anytime in 1933. July 4 is a critical date in US history and on this date Sun is at 14 Cancer, which in itself has wider implications in US history. By commencing the Silver futures on July 5, it is close to July 4 and Sun is close to 14 Cancer.

Jupiter / natal Sun

In April 2011, Silver prices reached a peak at just under $50 per ounce. Transiting Jupiter was making a 90 degree aspect to natal Sun at the time. From this peak, Silver prices declined towards a significant low in late 2015. Along the way, transiting Jupiter made a 0 degree conjunction to natal Sun in the August 2013 timeframe. Silver prices behaved extremely erratically during this period. During October, November and December 2016, Jupiter made a 90 degree hard aspect to the natal Sun position. The price chart in Figure 66 illustrates this transit. Note that the start of this transit commenced with a sharp rally from $17 to $19/oz. Prices then collapsed to $15.50. The exact end of this collapse came just as the Jupiter transit wrapped up. Co-incidence you say? I say not. If these price moves appear small, remember a $1 move on Silver is $5000 per contract traded.

The next hard aspect of Jupiter to natal Sun will not occur until 2020, in time for the end of the Gann Master Cycle and ensuing market weakness.

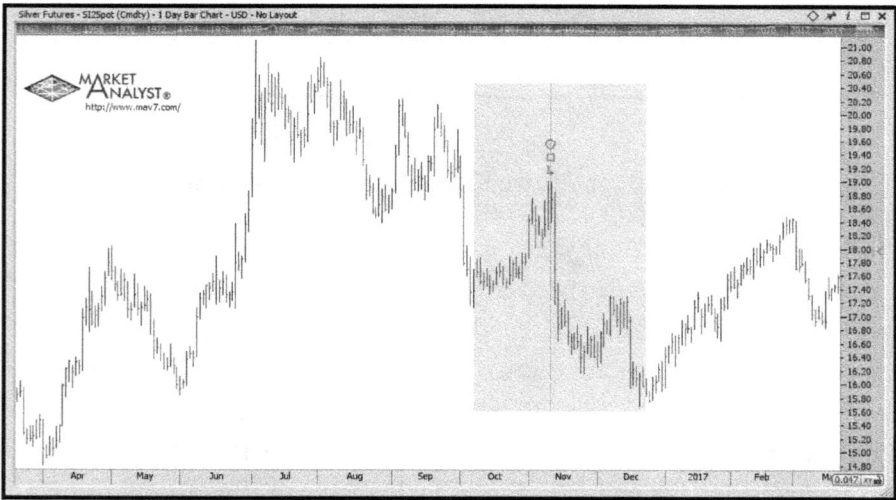

Figure 66 Silver futures and Jupiter / natal Sun

Sun / natal Sun

The daily Silver price chart in Figure 67 has been overlaid with times when transiting Sun makes 0, 90 and 180 degree aspects to the natal Sun position at 12 Cancer. Note how these events bear a good alignment to price inflection points. Using a suitable measure of trend change (ie one of Wilder's methods), one would implement a trade during these Sun/natal Sun aspects if the trend recorded a change. Note that it is also possible for a Sun/natal Sun aspect to cause an existing trend to accelerate.

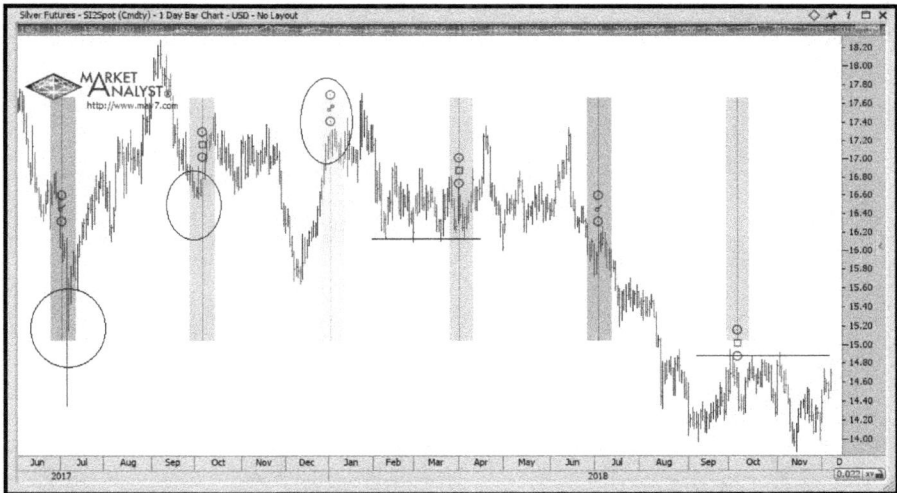

Figure 67 Silver and Sun/natal Sun events

For 2019, Sun will make aspects to natal Sun as follows:

December 27, 2018 – January 8, 2019: Sun 180 degrees to natal Sun

March 25-April 7: Sun will pass 90 degrees to natal Sun

June 26-July 10: Sun will pass 0 degrees to natal Sun.

September 28-October 10: Sun passes 90 degrees to natal Sun.

Mars / natal Sun

The Silver price chart in Figure 68 has been overlaid with times when transiting Mars makes 0, 90 and 180 degree aspects to the natal Sun position. Using a suitable measure of trend change (ie one of Wilder's methods), one would implement a trade during these Mars/natal Sun aspects if the trend recorded a change. Notice in this chart that the low recorded in June 2017 came just as a Mars conjunct natal Sun aspect was wrapping up.

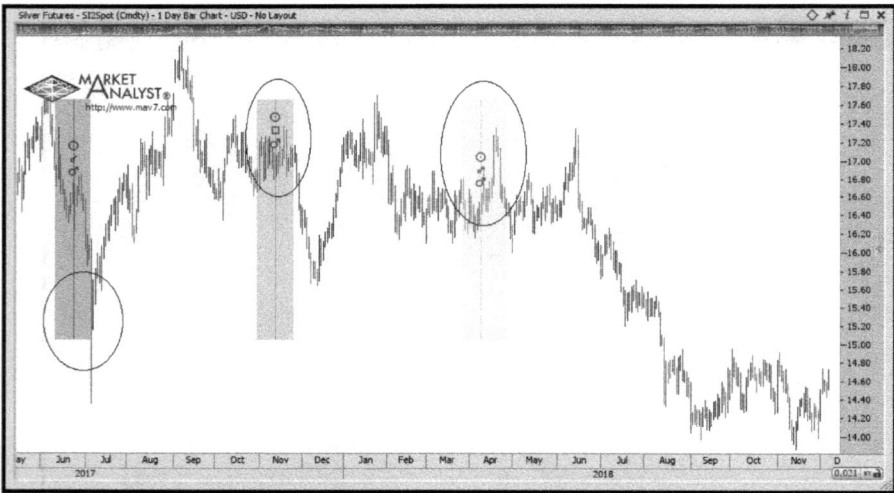

Figure 68 Silver and Mars/natal Sun events

For 2019, Mars will make aspects to natal Sun as follows:

January 10 – January 30: Mars will pass 90 degrees to natal Sun.

May 25– June 14: Mars will pass 0 degrees to natal Sun.

October 14- November 1: Mars will pass 90 degrees to natal Sun.

Declination

Planetary declinations should also be considered when studying price action of Silver futures. In particular the declination maxima and minima of Venus and also of Sun should be watched. Why Venus? As it turns out, Venus had just made its maximum declination in 1933 as Silver futures were starting to trade for the very first time. This was a very strong hint to me that Venus declination should be examined relative to Silver price inflections. Figures 69 and Figure 70 illustrate the effect of both Venus and Sun declination events. In 2018, Silver prices made what amounted to a double top formation at just over $17 in the April-June period which aligned with the beginning and end of a Venus declination maxima occurrence. The second of these tops aligned perfectly to the Sun at maximum declination (Summer Solstice). As maxima and minima in declination draw near, use a suitable trend change indicator to assist you in your decision making.

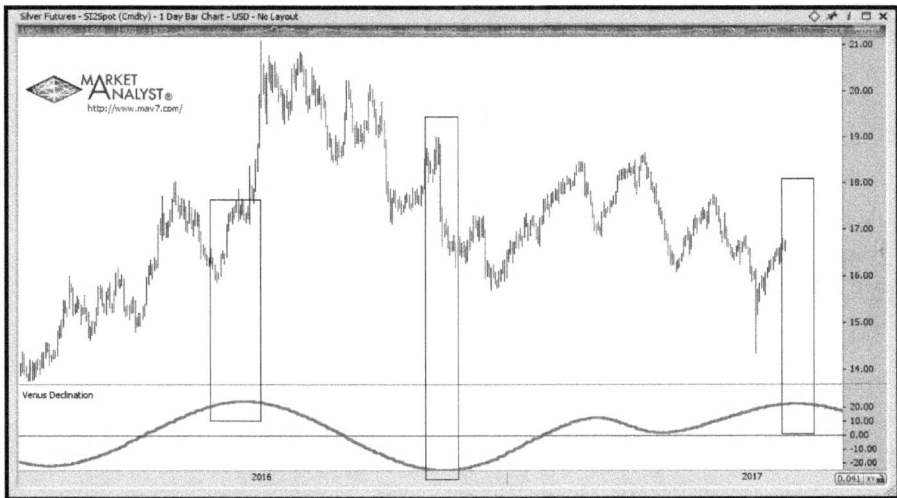

Figure 69 Venus Declination and Silver prices

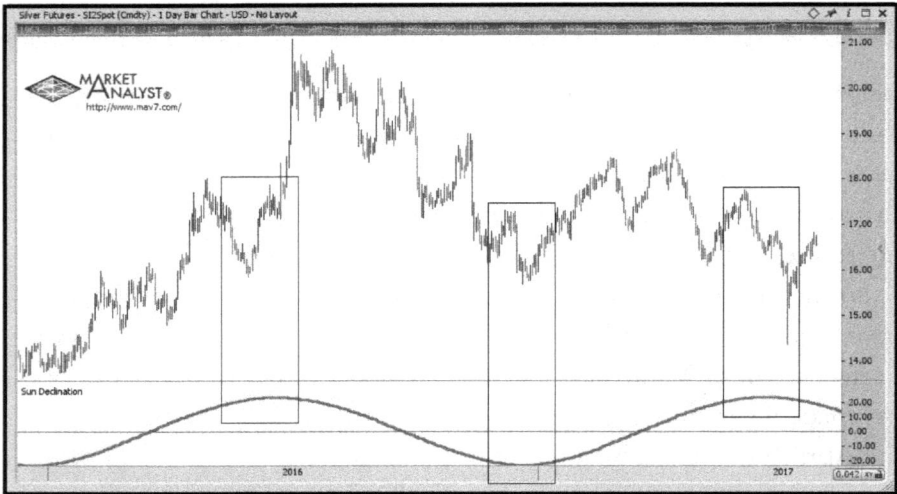

Figure 70 Sun Declination and Silver prices

For 2019, Sun will be at its maximum declination at the Summer Solstice on June 21. Sun will at its minimum declination at the Winter Solstice on December 21.

For 2019, Venus will exhibit its maximum declination from mid-June through mid-July. It will be interesting to see how this factors in with the natal Sun location at 12 Cancer which falls right in the middle of this declination maxima event.

Copper

The First Trade Date for Copper futures was July 29, 1988. Figure 71 illustrates the First Trade horoscope in geocentric format.

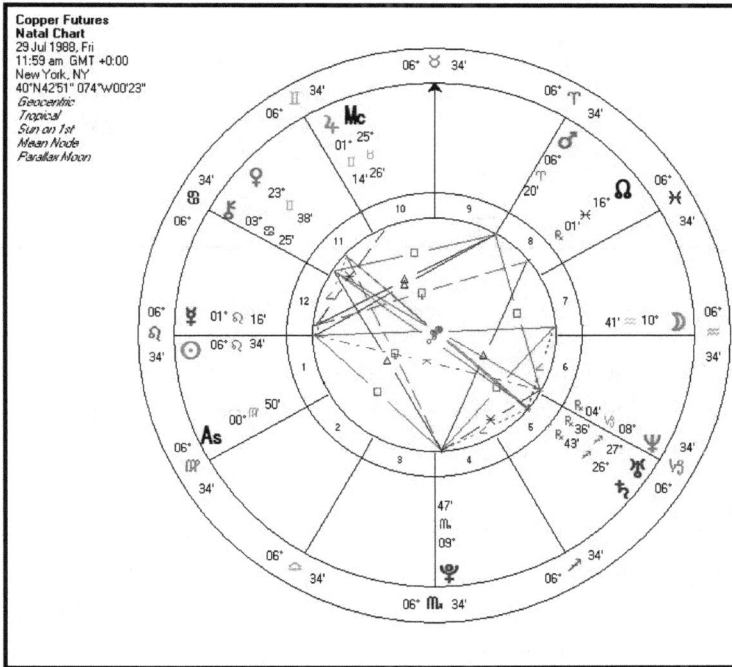

Figure 71 Copper futures First Trade horoscope

This horoscope wheel features an Inferior Conjunction of Mercury in the sign of Leo. Note also that Moon is in Aquarius. Recall from Chapter 1 that I noted during the Renaissance period, dreams were said to come true if Moon was in Aquarius. Whether this bit of arcane history factored into the selection of July 29, 1988 as the First Trade date remains uncertain. But I would not be shocked to learn that there is a connection.

Also, notice in this horoscope that the First Trade date is that of a Full Moon.

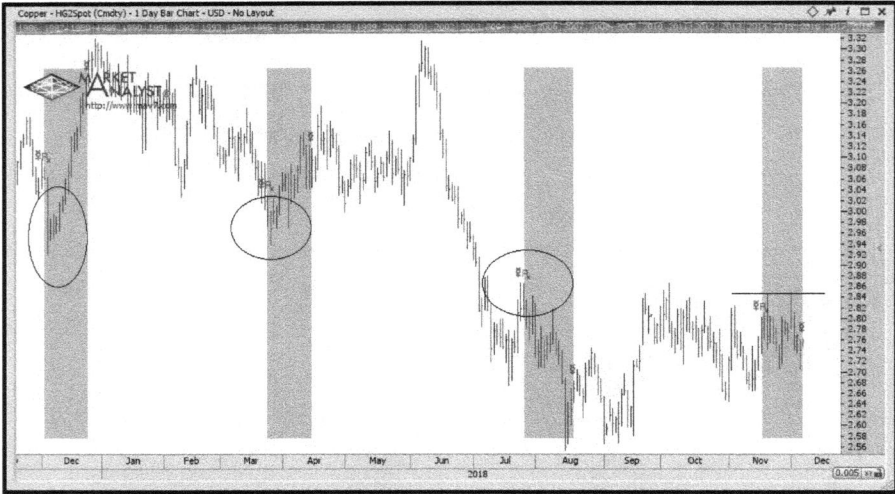

Figure 72 Copper and Mercury retrograde events

An Inferior Conjunction of Mercury marks the start of a new Mercury cycle around the Sun. Mercury Inferior Conjunction events always occur in association with Mercury being retrograde.

The daily price chart for Copper futures in Figure 72 has been overlaid with Mercury retrograde events. Knowing that such an event is approaching, one should watch a suitable price chart technical indicator for evidence of a short term trend change. Note that at the far right of this chart, Copper prices are just emerging from a retrograde event.

For 2019, Mercury will be:

➤ In retrograde from March 5 through March 27.

➤ In retrograde from July 7 through July 31.

➤ In retrograde from October 31 through November 19.

Canadian Dollar, British Pound and Japanese Yen

These three futures instruments all started trading on May 16th, 1972 at the Chicago Mercantile Exchange. The horoscope in Figure 73 illustrates planetary placements at this date. It is interesting to note that Mars is 180 degrees opposite Jupiter. This suggests that Mars and Jupiter may play a role in price fluctuations on these currencies. Mars is also 0 degrees conjunct to Venus, suggesting another cyclical relationship.

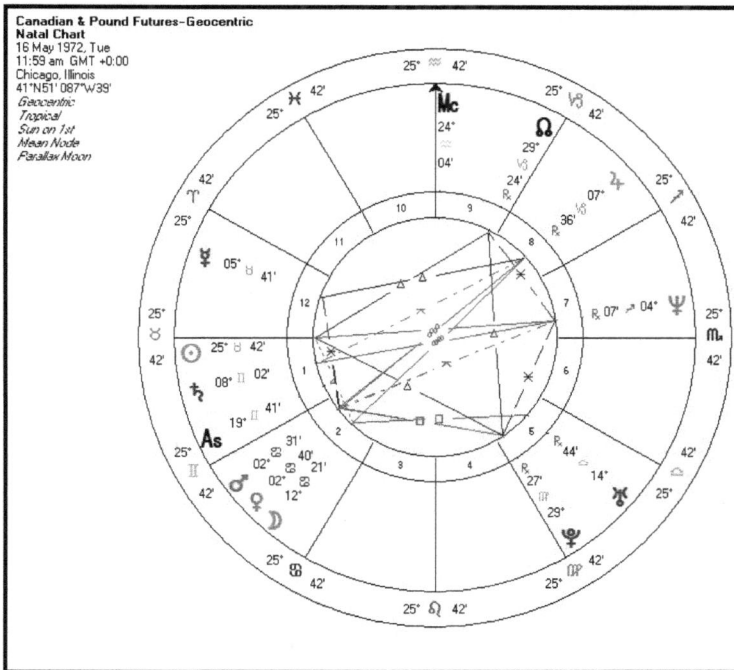

Figure 73 Pound, Yen, Canadian First Trade horoscope

The Mars Influence

The chart in Figure 74 illustrates price action on the Canadian Dollar. Mars conjunct Venus events only occur every couple years. As this chart shows, such an event occurred in early 2015 and as it did, the Canadian Dollar registered a low and a change of trend. Another conjunction in late 2015 resulted in an acceleration of the existing downward trend.

The next such Mars/Venus event will come in August 2019.

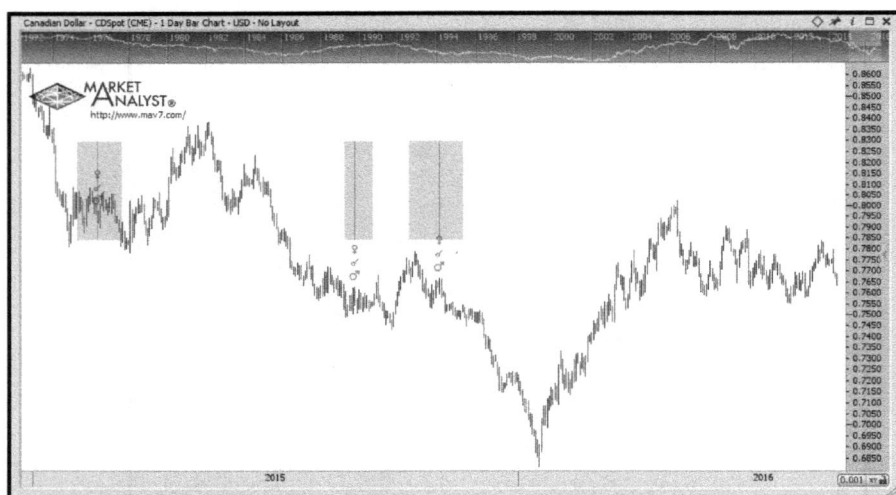

Figure 74 Canadian Dollar Mars conjunct Venus

Natal Transits

Transiting Sun passing natal Sun, natal Mars and natal Jupiter are events that currency traders may wish to focus on.

To illustrate, the chart in Figure 75 illustrates the effect on the British Pound of transiting Sun passing natal Mars (2 degrees of Cancer in the 1972 horoscope chart) and Sun passing natal Sun (25 of Taurus in the 1972 horoscope). Although not shown on this chart, in mid-2016 at the British Brexit Vote, the Pound took a drubbing and the plunge came right at a Sun / natal Mars conjunction. Not every such transit aligns to a such violent trend swings, but all such transits should be watched nonetheless.

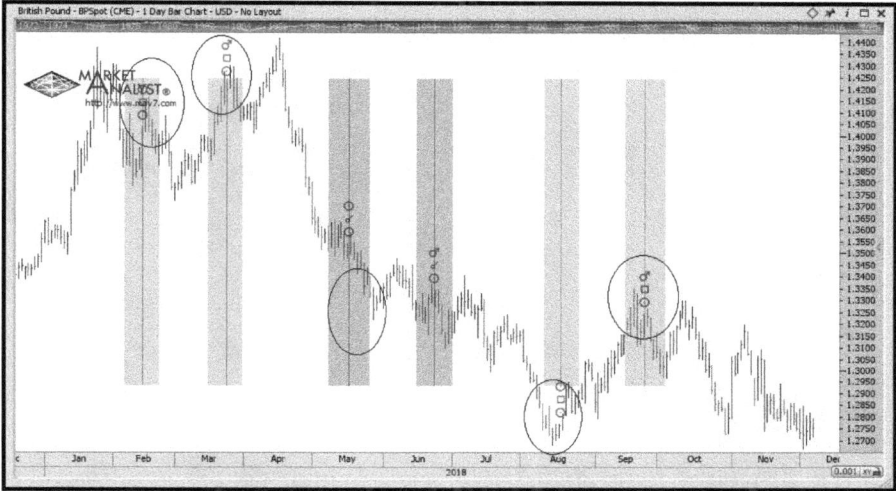

Figure 75 British Pound and Sun passing natal Mars & natal Sun

The chart in Figure 76 illustrates the effect on the Canadian Dollar of transiting Sun passing natal Jupiter. The correlations are uncanny in their alignment.

For 2019, transiting Sun will make hard aspects to the natal Mars point of 2 degrees Cancer as follows:

March 16 to March 28: 90 degrees square

June 16 to June 29: 0 degrees conjunct

September 17 to September 30: 90 degrees square

December 16 to December 30: 180 degrees opposite

For 2019, transiting Sun will make hard aspects to the natal Sun point of 25 Taurus as follows:

February 7 to February 21: 90 degrees square

May 8 to May 24: 0 degrees conjunct

August 10 to August 27: 90 degrees square

November 10 to November 26: 180 degrees opposite

For 2019, transiting Sun will make hard aspects to the natal Jupiter point of 7 degrees Capricorn as follows:

March 20 to April 2: 90 degrees square

June 21 to July 5: 10 degrees opposite

September 22 to October 7: 90 degrees square

December 21 to January 4, 2020: 0 degrees conjunct

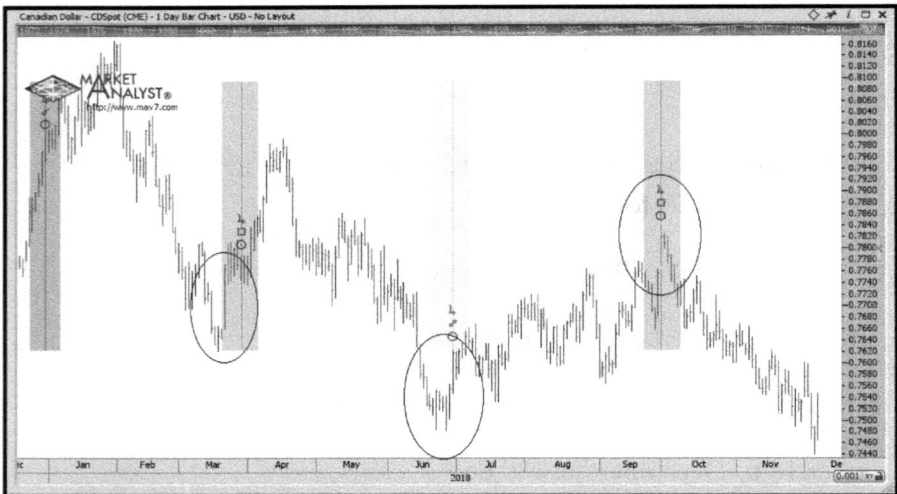

Figure 76 Canadian Dollar Sun conjunct natal Jupiter

Mercury Retrograde

Currency traders should pay close attention to Mercury retrograde events as they can bear a good alignment to trend changes on the Pound, Yen and Canadian Dollar.

The Canadian Dollar price chart in Figure 77 has been overlaid with Mercury retrograde events. Traders are advised to use a suitable trend change chart indicator to watch for actionable trend changes during retrograde events.

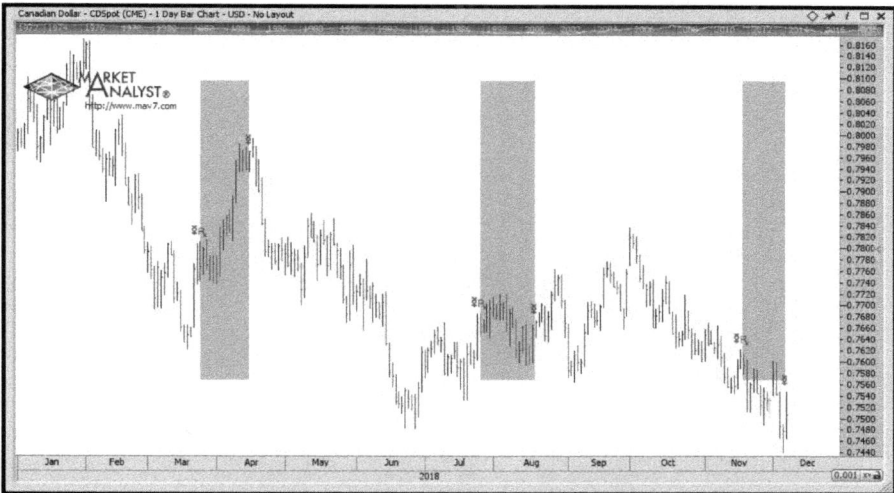

Figure 77 Canadian Dollar and Mercury retrograde

For 2019, Mercury will be:

➢ In retrograde from March 5 through March 27.

➢ In retrograde from July 7 through July 31.

➢ In retrograde from October 31 through November 19.

Euro Currency Futures

The Euro became the official currency for the European Union on January 1, 2002 when Euro bank notes became freely and widely circulated. Arguably there may be another date – January 1999 when the E.U. zone nations were required to establish a fixed rate of exchange between their currencies and the Euro currency. But, I prefer the 2002 date because of the conjunct relation between Venus and Sun. The First Trade horoscope for the 2002 date in Figure 78 reveals Sun and Venus are conjunct in Capricorn.

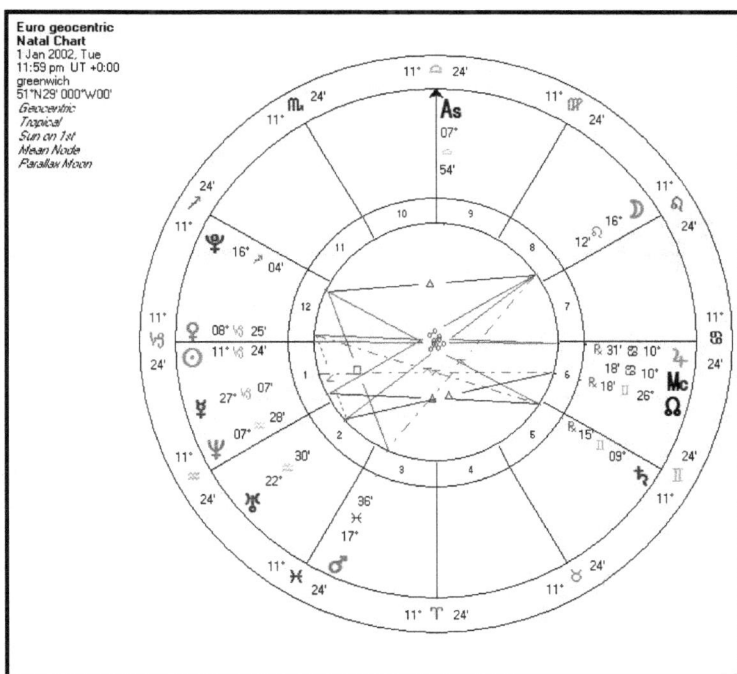

Figure 78 Euro Currency First Trade horoscope

The chart of the Euro currency in Figure 79 has been overlaid with Venus / Sun conjunct events. The narrow bars are times when Venus was retrograde and can be left out of any consideration. Notice how the Euro lost significant value in 2016 following a conjunction, which by the way aligned to the Brexit vote. A similar downdraft has been in place following the conjunction in early 2018.

The next Sun / Venus conjunction will be mid-July through mid-August 2019.

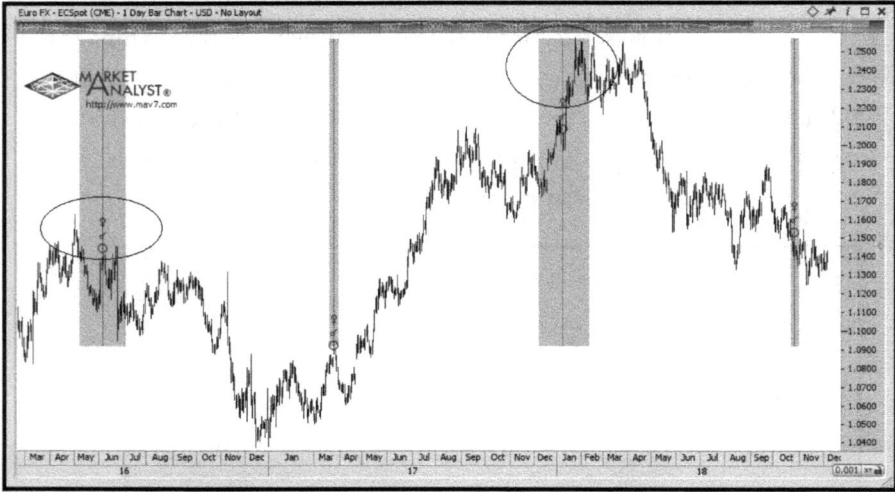

Figure 79 Sun / Venus Conjunction and the Euro

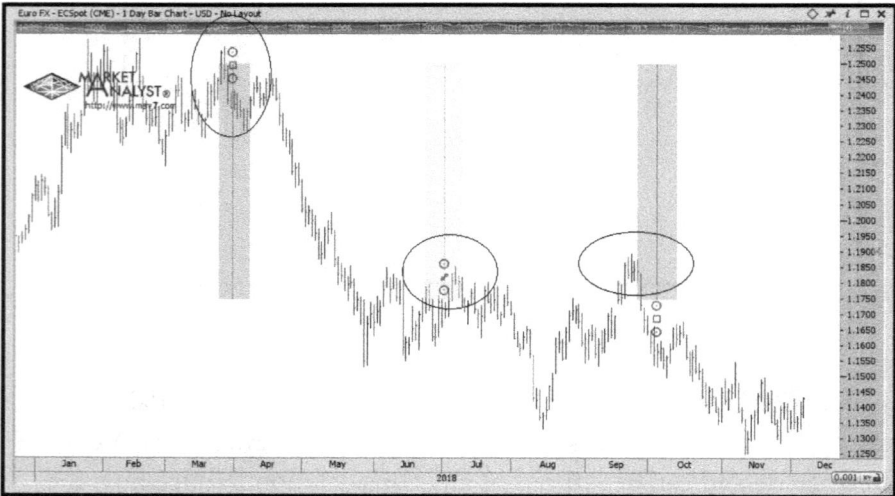

Figure 80 - Natal Transits and the Euro Currency

Natal Transits

The chart in Figure 80 has been overlaid with events of transiting Sun making 0, 90 and 180 degree aspects to the natal Sun position in the Euro 2002 First Trade horoscope. Sun/natal Sun aspects can and often do align to inflection points on the Euro. In 2018 notice how the three transits all were followed with down-trending price action.

For 2019, transiting Sun will be:

Completing a 0 degree conjunction to natal Sun during the first week of January.

90 degrees to natal Sun March 26 through April 7.

180 degrees opposite natal Sun from June 22 through July 12.

90 degrees to natal Sun from 28 of September through October 9.

Australian Dollar

Australian dollar futures started trading on the Chicago Mercantile Exchange on January 13, 1987. As the horoscope in Figure 81 shows, Sun and Mercury are at a Superior Conjunction at 22-23 degrees Capricorn.

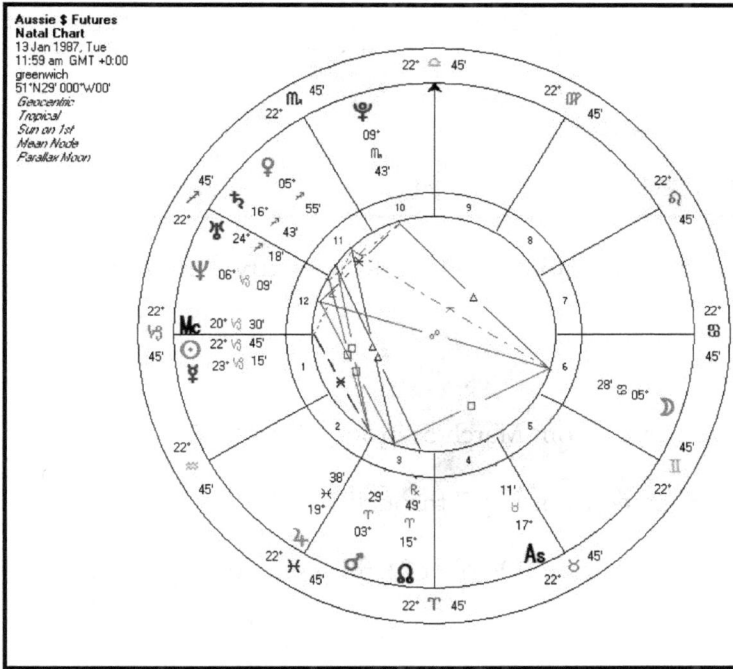

Figure 81 First Trade horoscope of Australian Dollar futures

Mercury Retrograde

Times when Mercury is retrograde should be considered if trading Australian Dollar futures. The chart in Figure 82 has been overlaid with Mercury retrograde events. These events often align to price inflection points.

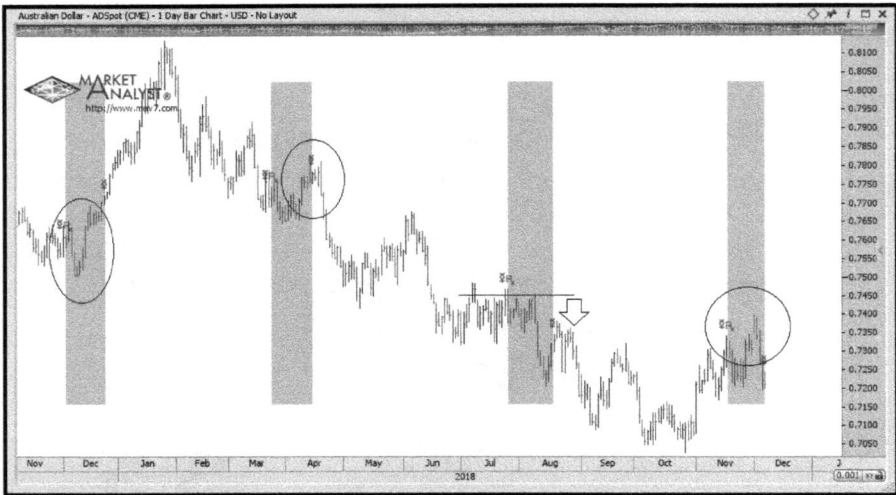

Figure 82 Australian Dollar and Mercury Conjunctions

For 2019, Mercury will be:

> ➤ In retrograde from March 5 through March 27.

> ➤ In retrograde from July 7 through July 31.

> ➤ In retrograde from October 31 through November 19.

Natal Transits

Transits to the natal Sun position of 22 Capricorn from the 1987 First
Trade horoscope can be used as tools to help one navigate the price
action of the Australian Dollar as the price chart in Figure 83 illustrates.
Note that in early 2018 a Sun / natal Sun conjunction came within 4
days of a significant high point, the likes of which has not been seen
since on the Australian Dollar. At that time the 14 period RSI was in
overbought territory and price action had extended beyond the usual
amount of deviation from the 55 day moving average thus offering the
trader a hint that a price reversal was in the cards. The Astrology helped
to pinpoint the timing.

Figure 83 Australian Dollar and Sun/natal Sun events

For 2019, transiting Sun will make 0, 90, and 180 degree aspects to natal Sun:

0 degrees to natal Sun from January 5 through January 21

90 degrees square to natal Sun from April 6 through April 18

180 degrees to natal Sun from July 6 through July 25

90 degrees to natal Sun from October 9 through October 21

30 Year Bond Futures

30 Year Bond futures started trading in Chicago on August 22, 1977.
Figure 84 presents the geocentric First Trade horoscope for this date.

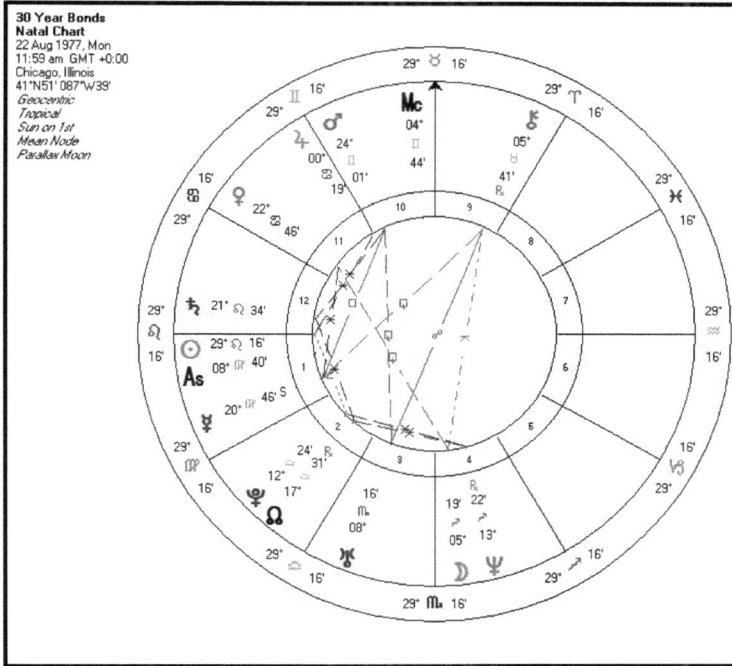

Figure 84 First Trade horoscope for 30 Year Bond futures

Natal Transits

My research has indicated that events of transiting Sun making 0, 90
and 180 degree aspects to the natal Jupiter position at 0 degrees Cancer
are valuable tools for the Bond trader. Traders of the 30 Year Bond
futures may wish to incorporate this information with a suitable
technical trend indicator into their trades. Figure 85 illustrates Bond
price performance with the Sun/natal Jupiter transits overlaid.

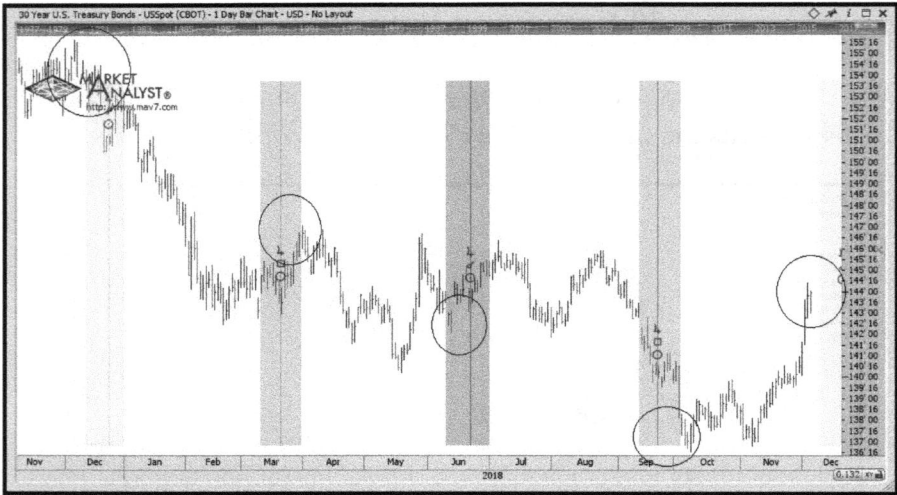

Figure 85 Bonds (30 Year) and Sun in aspect to natal Jupiter

For 2019, transiting Sun will make hard 0, 90 or 180 degree aspects to natal Jupiter as follows:

At January 1, a 180 degree aspect will just be wrapping up. Given the current strong uptrend, a reversion to the mean would not be out of the question in the coming Sun/natal Jupiter transit.

March 14 through March 29, transiting Sun will make a 90 degree aspect

June 12 through July 1, transiting Sun will make a 0 degree aspect.

September 17 through September 30, transiting Sun will make a 90 degree aspect.

December 14 through December 29, transiting Sun will be completing a 180 degree hard aspect.

Mercury Retrograde

Look closely at the First Trade horoscope in Figure 84 and you will note that the position of Mercury (at 20 Virgo) is further delineated by a letter S. This letter denotes *stationary* and curiously enough this First Trade date of August 22, 1977 comes one day prior to Mercury turning retrograde. Therein lies a strong hint. The price chart in Figure 86 has been overlaid with Mercury retrograde events. Note the propensity for short term inflections in trend at these retrograde events.

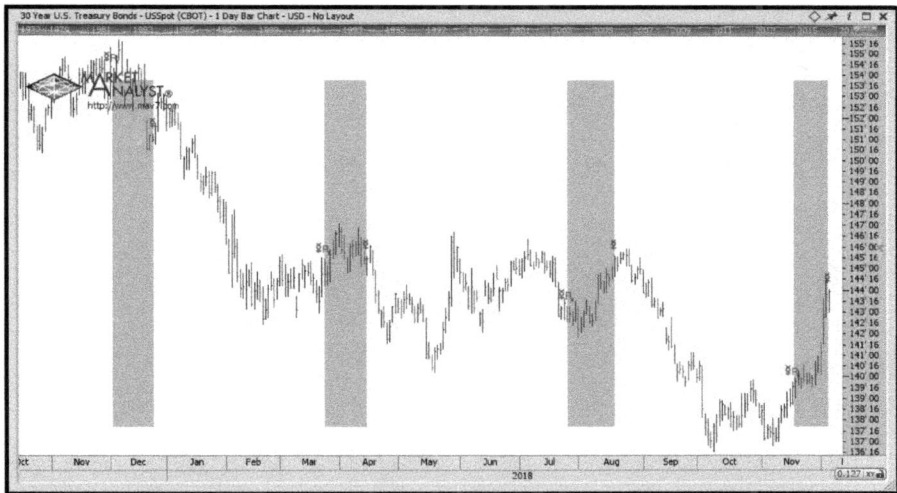

Figure 86   30 Year Bonds and Mercury retrograde

For 2019, Mercury will be:

➢ In retrograde from March 5 through March 27.

➢ In retrograde from July 7 through July 31.

➢ In retrograde from October 31 through November 19.

10 Year Treasury Note Futures

10 Year Treasury Notes started trading in Chicago on May 3, 1982. Figure 87 presents the geocentric First Trade horoscope for this date.

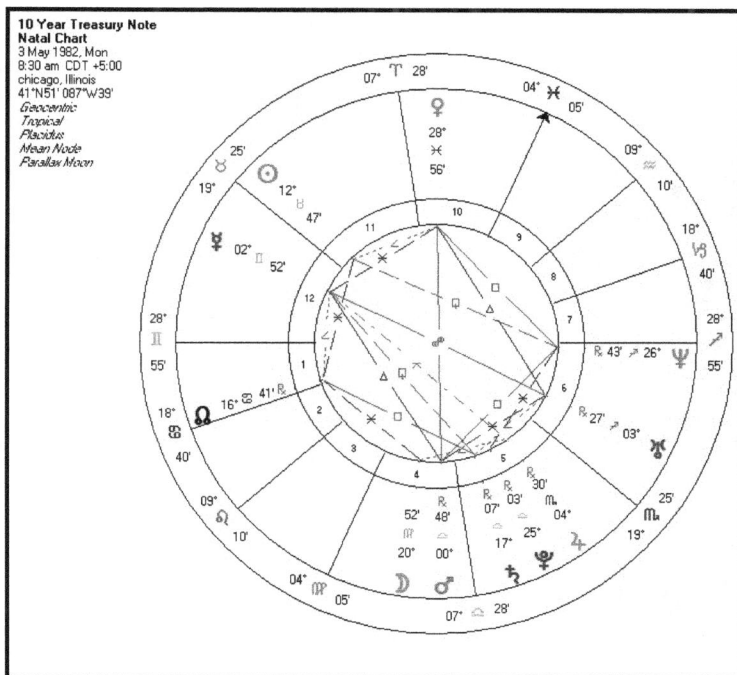

Figure 87 First Trade horoscope for 10 Year Treasury Notes

Retrograde

Notice in the First Trade horoscope in Figure 87, that Mars is denoted Rx which stands for retrograde. Therein rests another valuable clue. Figure 88 illustrates what happened in 2018 at a Mars retrograde event. Mercury retrograde events also bear watching when following price action on the 10 Year Treasury Notes. Figure 89 illustrates the connection between price inflection points and Mercury retrograde.

In 2019, Mars will not be retrograde. It will retrograde again in 2020 in time for the end of the Gann Master Cycle.

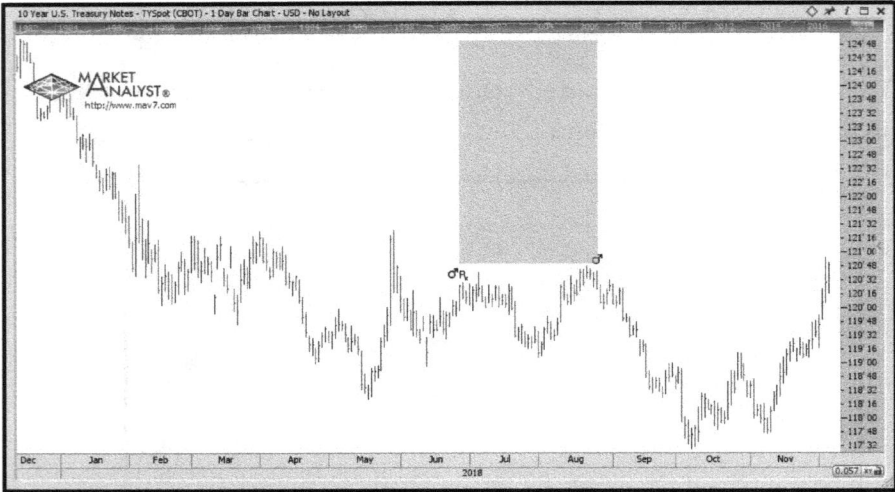

Figure 88 Mars retrograde and 10 Year Treasuries

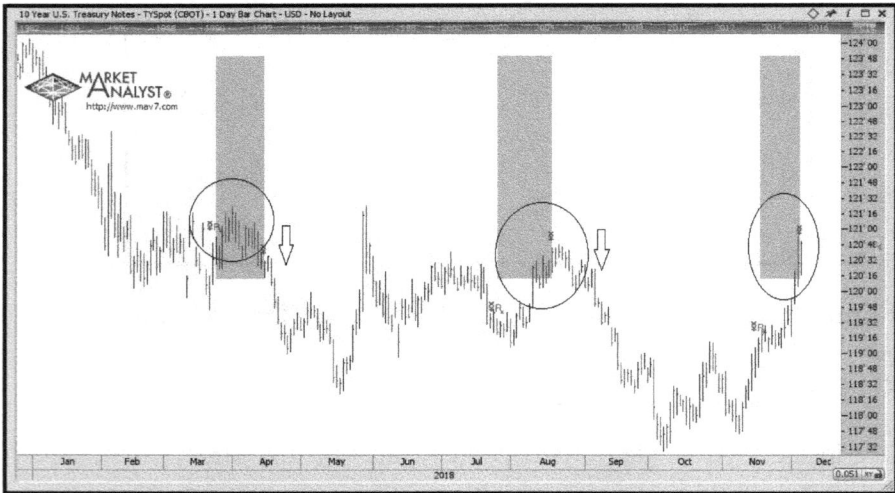

Figure 89 Mercury retrograde and 10 Year Treasuries

For 2019, Mercury will be:

> ➢ In retrograde from March 5 through March 27.

> ➢ In retrograde from July 7 through July 31.

> ➢ In retrograde from October 31 through November 19.

Wheat, Corn, Oats

Wheat, Corn and Oats futures all share the same first trade date from 1877. The horoscope in Figure 90 shows planetary placements at this date.

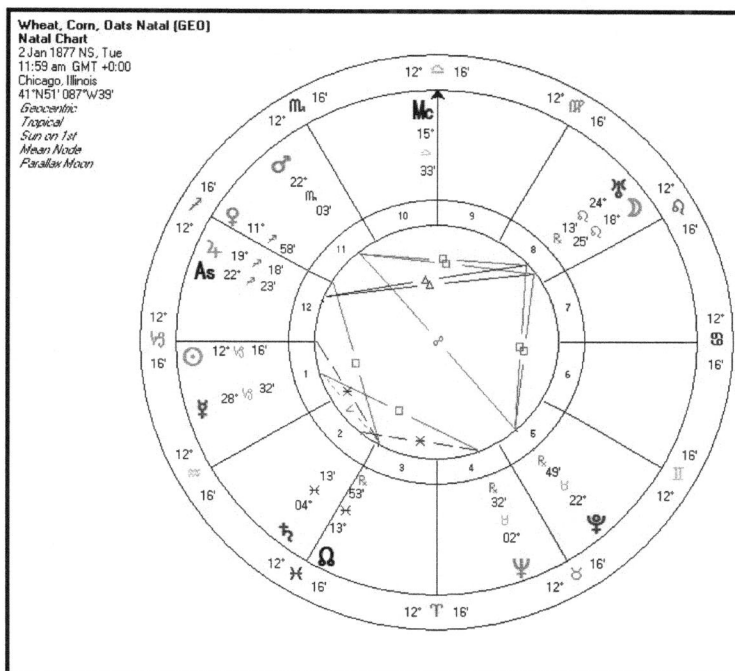

Figure 90 First Trade horoscope for Wheat, Corn and Oats futures

Over the past couple years, my incessant reading and research has revealed that W.D. Gann was also known to follow a First Trade horoscope wheel from April 3, 1848, the date the Chicago Board of Trade was founded. Figure 91 shows this horoscope wheel.

In the 1877 Wheat/Corn natal horoscope, the Sun is at 12 Capricorn, exactly square to the location of Sun in the above shown 1848 horoscope.

In the 1877 chart, the Descendant is at 12 Cancer. Look where Jupiter is in this 1848 chart – within 0.5 degrees of 12 Cancer. Co-incidence you say? I rather doubt it.

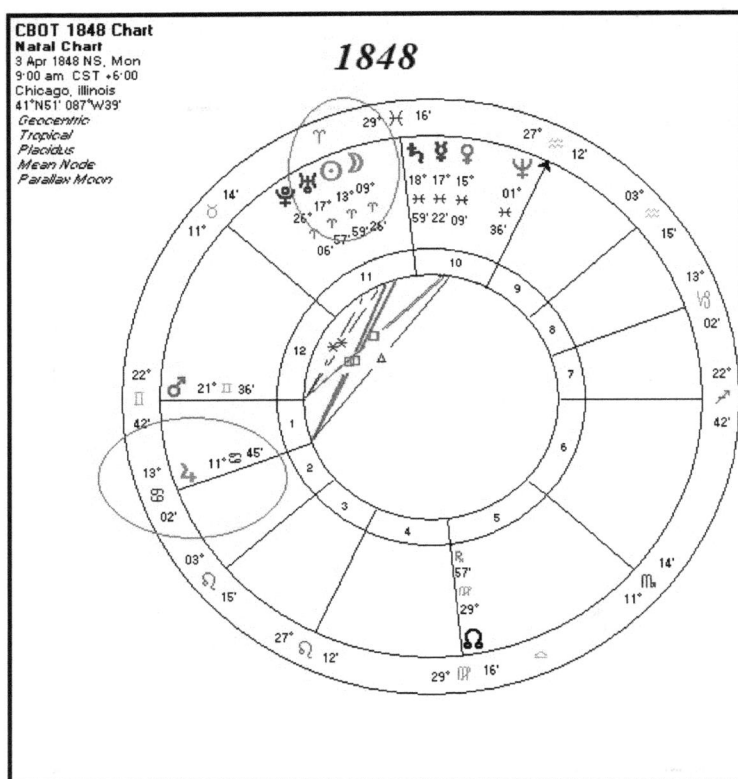

Figure 91 1848 First Trade horoscope for CBOT

Natal Aspects to Both Horoscopes

Events of transiting Sun making 0, 90 and 180 degree aspects to the natal Sun position in the 1877 First Trade horoscope or the 1848 CBOT natal horoscope can be used as a tool to guide traders through the price volatility of Wheat, Corn and Oats. Because of the peculiar alignment of these two horoscopes, a 0 degree conjunction to natal Sun in the 1877 horoscope will be a 90 degree square to the natal Sun of the

1848 horoscope.

Figure 92 illustrates the effect on Corn prices of transiting Sun making hard aspects to the natal Sun position. Note how the significant low in mid-2018 came right at a Sun / natal Sun aspect.

Figure 92 Corn prices and Sun/natal Sun events

Mars is also a planet to keep tabs on. Figure 93 illustrates transiting Mars making hard aspects to the natal Sun position. The application of a chart technical indicator to monitor short term trend changes is essential to properly utilizing these natal transits. In mid-2017 a Mars / natal Sun transit was within days of aligning to a significant price reversal point. In late 2017 a Mars / natal Sun aspect marked a floor of support. In April 2018 price reacted erratically during the transit.

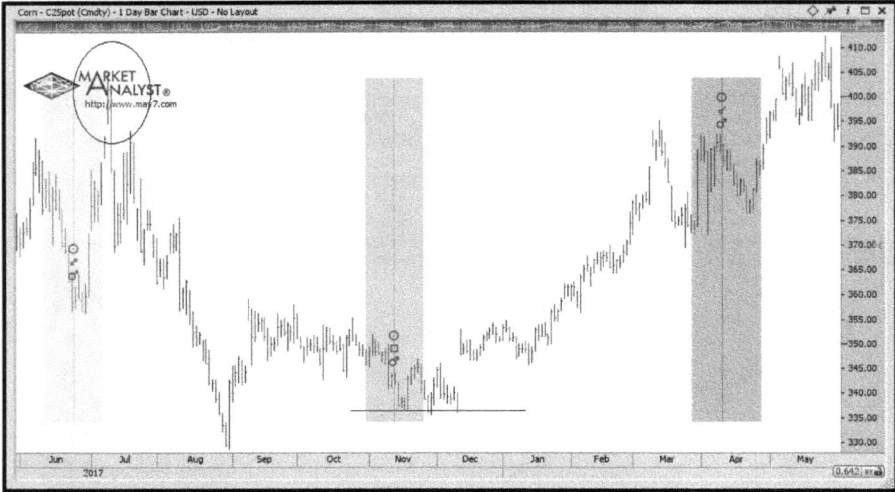

Figure 93 Corn prices and Mars/natal Sun events

For 2019, transiting Sun will be 0 degree to the 1877 natal Sun from January 1 through January 8. (90 degrees to the 1848 natal Sun).

Sun will be 90 degrees natal Sun from March 27 through April 8. (0 degrees to the 1848 natal Sun).

Sun will be 180 degrees natal Sun from June 26 through July 11. (90 degrees to the 1848 natal Sun).

Sun will be 90 degrees natal Sun from September 29 through October 11. (180 degrees to the 1848 natal Sun)

For 2019, Mars will be 90 degrees to the 1877 natal Sun from January 10 through the end of January. (0 degrees to the 1848 horoscope).

Mars will be 180 degrees to the 1877 natal Sun from May 27 through June 14.

Mars will be 90 degrees to the 1877 natal Sun from October 16 through November 1.

Declination

Planetary declination also is a powerful tool that can be used to help traders identify the coming of trend reversals. Figures 94 and 95 illustrate the application of declination to Corn and Wheat price charts. If price has been rising (falling) and appears to be reaching what could be deemed an overbought (oversold) situation, check the declination level of Venus. If the declination is reaching an extreme or about to cross the zero level, you may find a trend reversal will soon make an appearance.

For 2019, Venus will record its declination maximum from mid-June through mid-July and its declination minimum from id-November through mid-December.

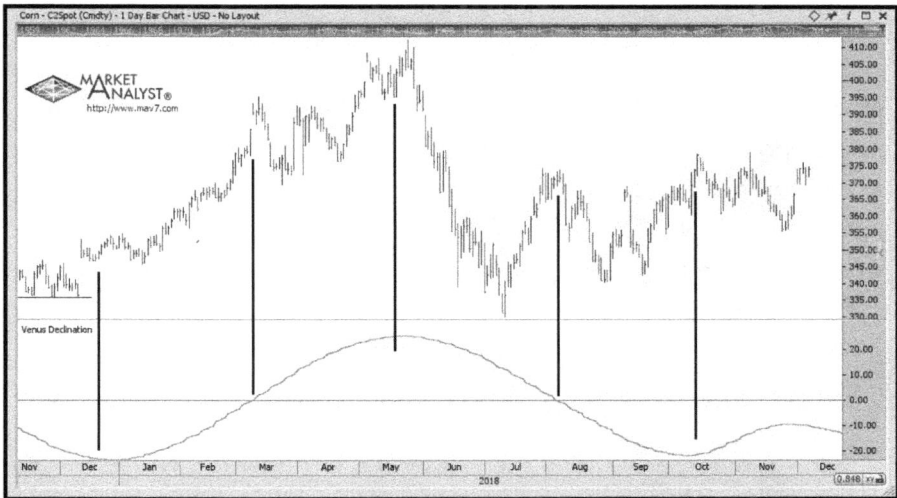

Figure 94 Corn prices and Mars Declination

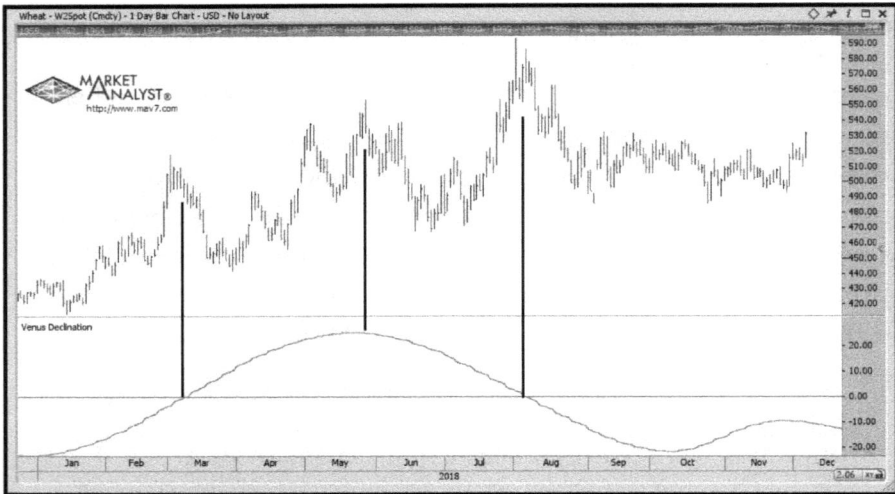

Figure 95 Wheat prices and Venus Declination

Retrograde

My research has also shown that Mercury retrograde plays a role in price pivot points on the grains. The price chart of Wheat futures in Figure 96 has been overlaid with Mercury retrograde events. Not all retrograde events will automatically align to a trend change. The propensity for such trend changes are however significant. The use of a suitable chart technical indicator is strongly recommended. Although not shown here, Mercury retrograde events do have a similar propensity to align to trend changes on Corn prices.

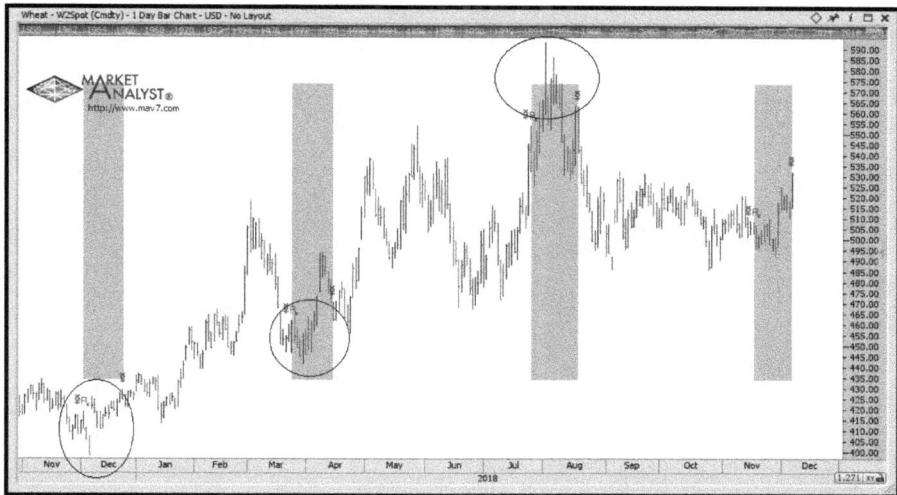

Figure 96 Wheat prices and Mercury retrograde events

For 2019, Mercury will be:

➢ In retrograde from March 5 through March 27.

➢ In retrograde from July 7 through July 31.

➢ In retrograde from October 31 through November 19.

Soybeans

Soybean futures started trading in Chicago on October 5, 1936. The horoscope in Figure 97 illustrates the planetary placements at that time. What I find intriguing is the location of the Sun. Notice how it is exactly 90 degrees to the location of the Sun in the First Trade horoscope for Wheat, Corn and Oats? Notice Sun is 180 degrees from the Sun in the 1848 CBOT natal chart? As I have previously suggested, the regulatory officials who determined these First Trade dates knew more about Astrology than you may think.

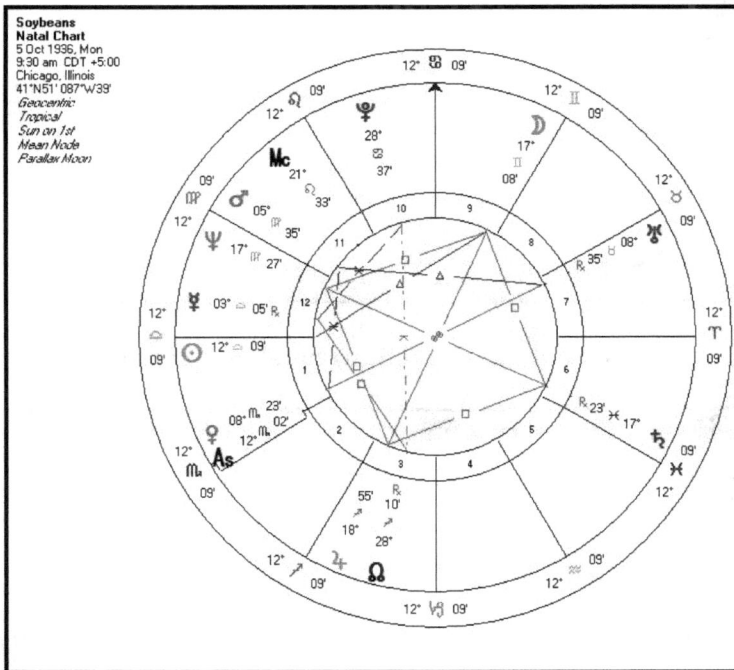

Figure 97 Soybeans First Trade horoscope

Natal Transits

Events of transiting Sun making 0, 90 and 180 degree aspects to the natal Sun position in the 1936 First Trade horoscope can be used to navigate the volatility of the Soybean market. Figure 98 illustrates the effect of transiting Sun making hard aspects to the natal Sun position. Figure 99 illustrates the effect of Mars making aspects to the natal Sun location. What I find intriguing is that the precipitous plunge in prices with the onset of the China trade spat started just as Venus was transiting 90 degrees to the natal Soybean Sun location.

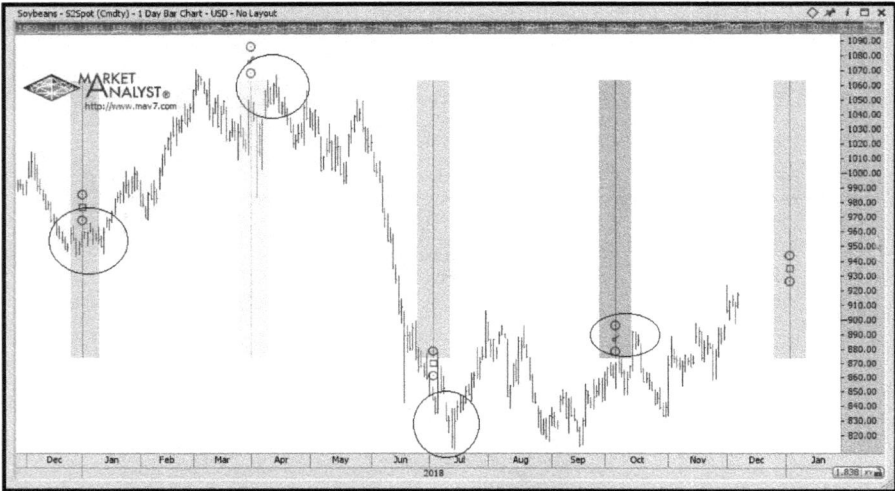

Figure 98 Soybeans and Sun/natal Sun events

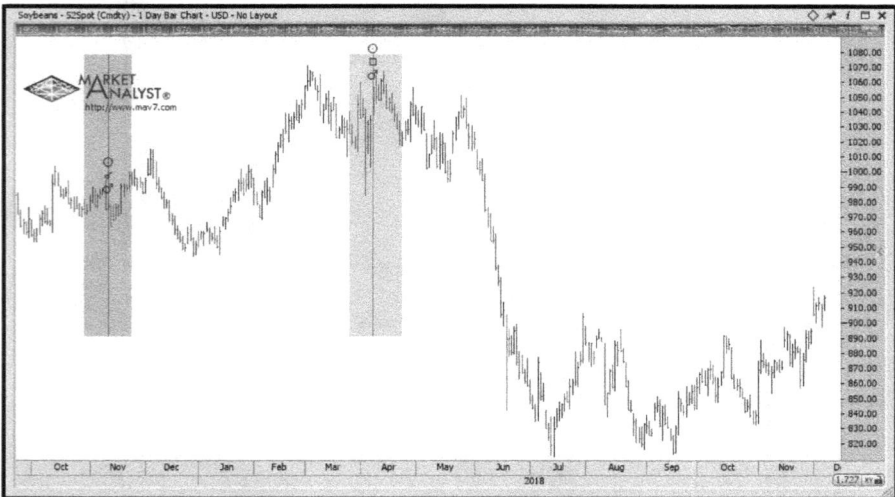

Figure 99 Soybeans and Mars/natal Sun events

For 2019, transiting Sun will make a 90 degree aspect to natal Sun from January 1 through January 8.

Transiting Sun will make a 180 degree aspect to natal Sun from March 25 through April 8.

A 90 degree aspect to natal Sun will occur from June 28 through July 11.

A 0 degree aspect will occur from September 26 through October 12.

For 2019, Mars will be 90 degrees to the 1877 natal Sun from January 10 through the end of January. (0 degrees to the 1848 horoscope).

Mars will be 180 degrees to the 1877 natal Sun from May 27 through June 14.

Mars will be 90 degrees to the 1877 natal Sun from October 16 through November 1.

Retrograde

Mercury retrograde events also contribute to the price behavior of Soybeans. The Soybeans chart in Figure 100 illustrates the Mercury retrograde effect. If there is a trend change associated with Mercury retrograde, the trend change may come immediately beforehand, during or immediately afterwards. The use of a suitable chart technical indicator is essential to help identify the trend shifts.

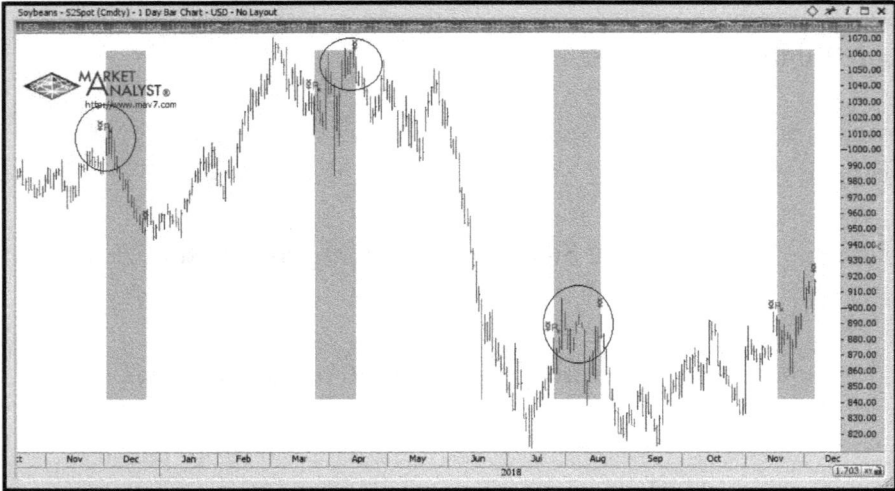

Figure 100 Soybeans and Mercury events

For 2019, Mercury will be:

➢ In retrograde from March 5 through March 27.

➢ In retrograde from July 7 through July 31.

➢ In retrograde from October 31 through November 19.

Declination

Soybeans also have a tendency to record price trend changes in proximity to Venus recording maximum, zero and minimum declinations. The Soybean price chart in Figure 101 illustrates further. Note that the precipitous trade-war fueled sell-off got underway right at the declination maxima in early June.

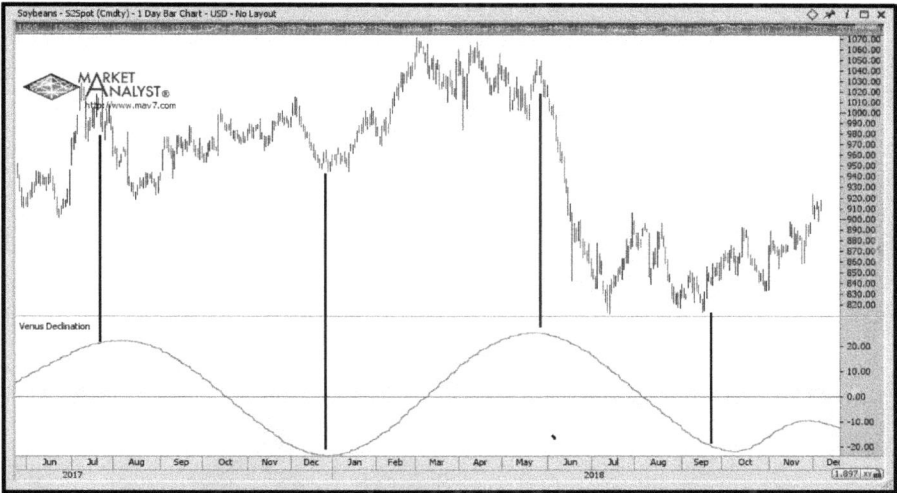

Figure 101 Soybeans and Venus Declination

For 2018, Venus will record its declination maxima from mid-June through mid-July and its minima from mid-November through mid-December.

Crude Oil

West Texas Intermediate Crude Oil futures started trading on a recognized exchange for the first time on March 30, 1983. A unique alignment of celestial points can be seen in the horoscope in Figure 102. Notice how Mars, North Node, (Saturn/Pluto/Moon) and Neptune conspire to form a rectangle.

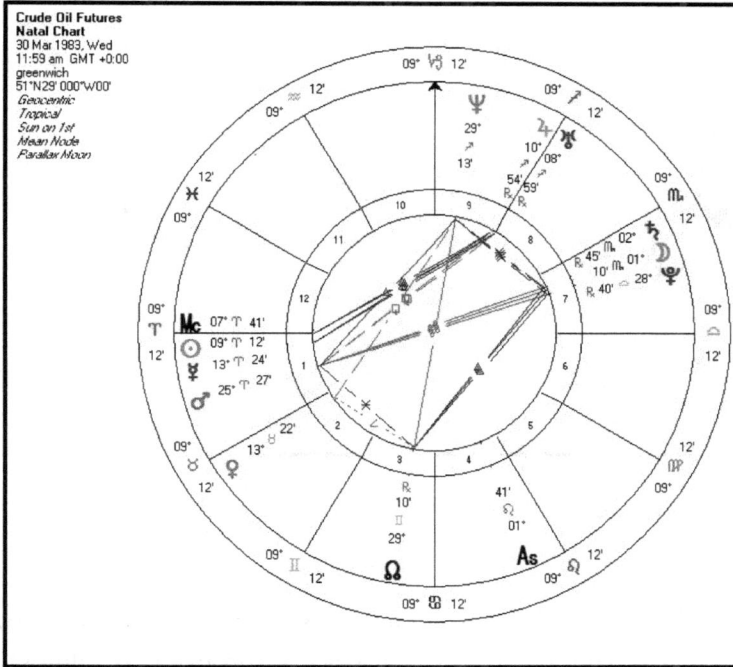

Figure 102 Crude Oil First Trade horoscope

Natal Transits

My experience has shown that Crude Oil is a complex instrument to analyze using Astrology. Given the peculiar rectangular shape that appears in the horoscope, my strategy for analyzing Crude Oil has been to use natal transits with a focus on transiting Sun and transiting Mars making 0 degree aspects to the four corner points of the rectangle.

The chart in Figure 103 illustrates Oil price action with events of Mars transiting the corners of the peculiar horoscope rectangle. The frightening lows of early 2016 came as Mars was passing the rectangle point denoted by Saturn/Moon. Two trend changes in 2017 aligned to transits of other rectangle corners.

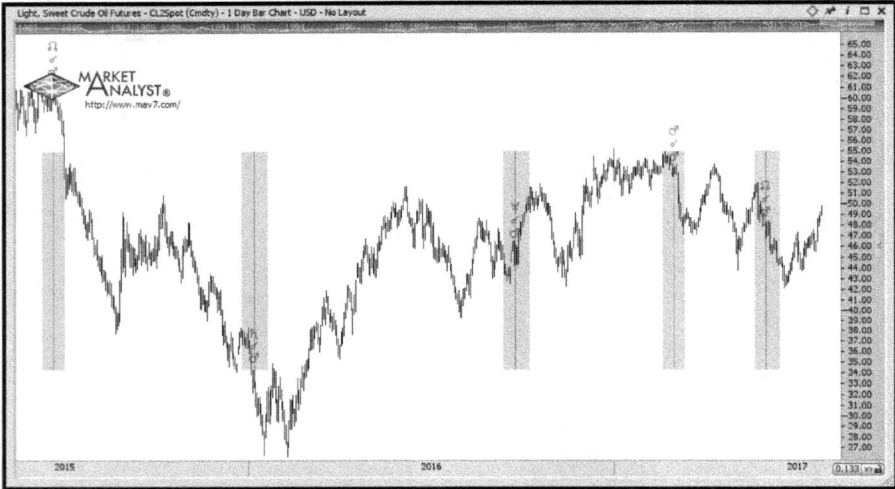

Figure 103 Crude Oil and Mars transits

Figure 104 illustrates events of Sun passing the rectangle corner positions in 2018. The key reversal in price came prior to (almost in anticipation of…) Sun transiting the corner of the rectangle containing Saturn. The alignment of these transits to swings and trend changes is remarkable.

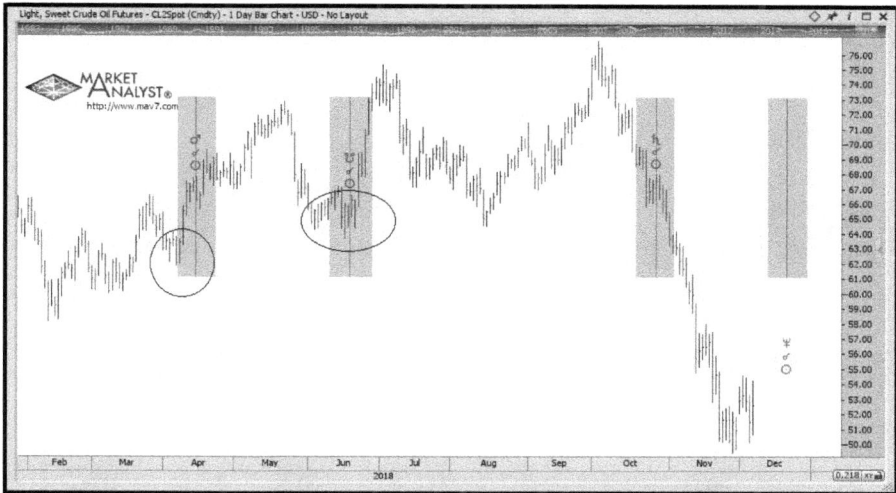

Figure 104 Crude Oil and Sun transits

For 2019, the four corners of the peculiar rectangle will be passed by as follows:

Sun will transit 0 degrees to the natal Mars location from April 9 through April 22.

Sun will transit 0 degrees to the natal Node location from June 7 through June 22.

Sun will transit 0 degrees to the natal (Saturn/Pluto/Moon) location from October 18 through November 1.

Sun will transit 0 degrees to the natal Neptune location from December 14 through the end of the year.

Mars will transit past the natal Mars location in the first two weeks of February.

Mars will transit past the natal Node location between May 7 and May 27.

Mars will transit past the natal Saturn location from the middle to end of November.

Retrograde

My studies have further shown that Crude Oil is influenced by Mercury retrograde and Venus retrograde as well. The Crude Oil price charts in Figure 105 and 106 illustrate this effect.

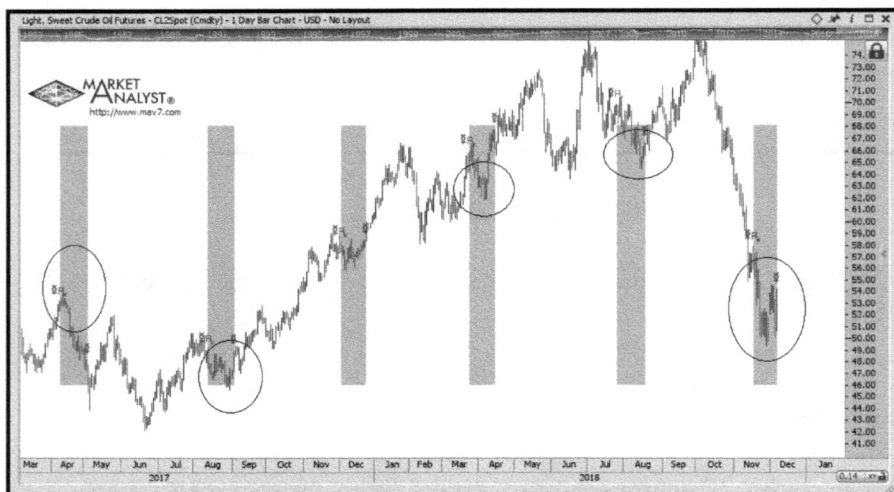

Figure 105 Crude Oil and Mercury retrograde events

For 2019, Mercury will be:

➤ In retrograde from March 5 through March 27.

➤ In retrograde from July 7 through July 31.

➤ In retrograde from October 31 through November 19.

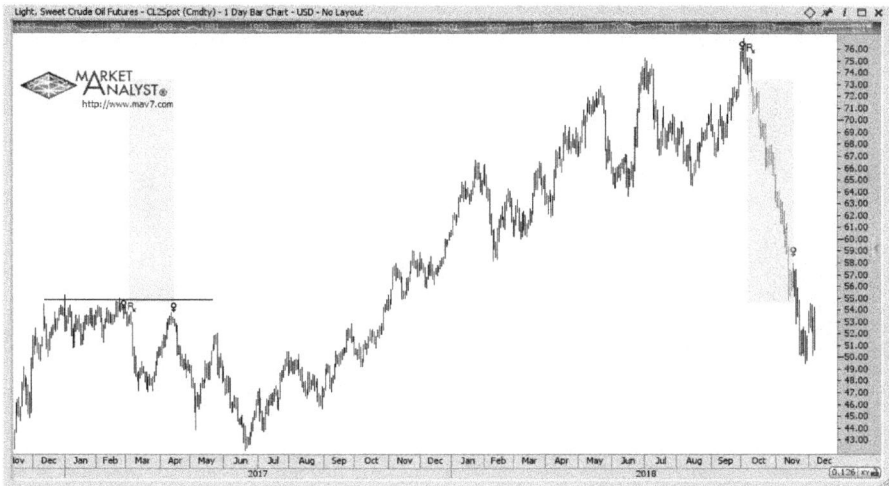

Figure 106 Crude Oil and Venus retrograde events

Note from the chart in Figure 106, Oil prices were hitting resistance in early 2017. A Venus retrograde event signalled the failure of price to get above resistance and the trend turned negative. In October 2018, the significant trend reversal came right at the start of a Venus retrograde event. Sun passing the natal Saturn corner of the horoscope rectangle formation than added fuel to the fire so to speak.

Cotton

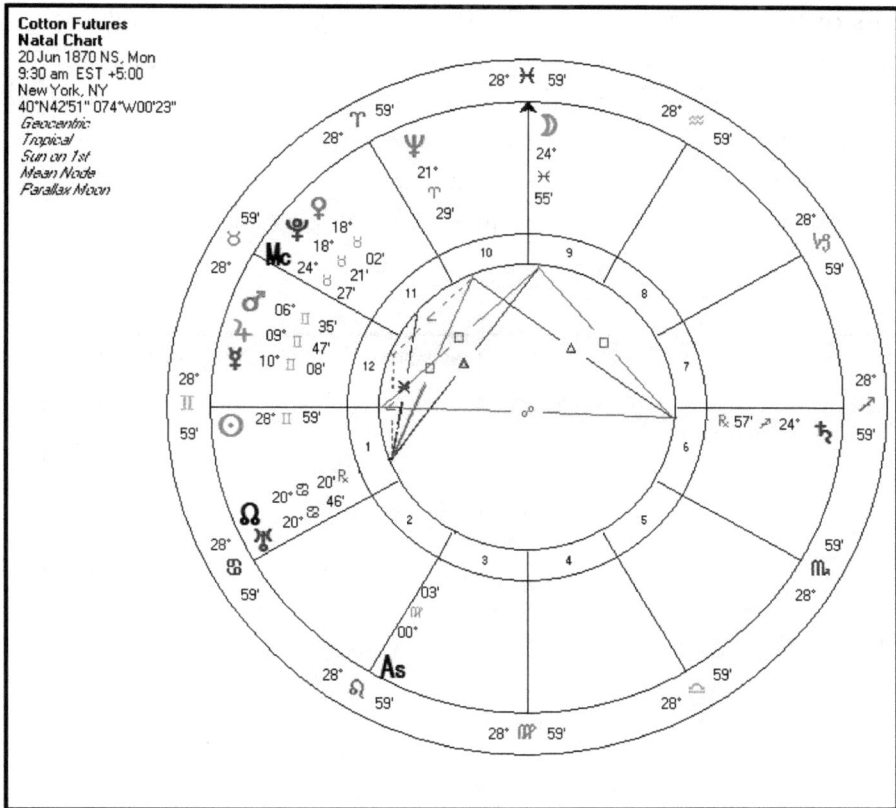

Figure 107   Cotton futures First Trade horoscope

After much painstaking research sifting through back-editions of New
York newspapers, I have come to conclude that Cotton futures first
started trading on June 20, 1870. The horoscope wheel in Figure 107
illustrates planetary placements at that time. At first glance, I find it
peculiar that the Moon is at the same degree and sign location (24
Pisces) as is the Mid-Heaven in the New York Stock Exchange natal
horoscope wheel from 1792. Surely this is no accident.

187

Natal Transits

Events of transiting Sun passing 0, 90 or 180 degrees to the natal Sun position are an effective tool for traders to use when navigating the choppy waters of Cotton prices. A suitable chart technical trend indicator is also a must. The Cotton price chart in Figure 108 illustrates further. Notice that the peak price and subsequent reversal in 2018 came mere days ahead of a Sun conjunct natal Sun event.

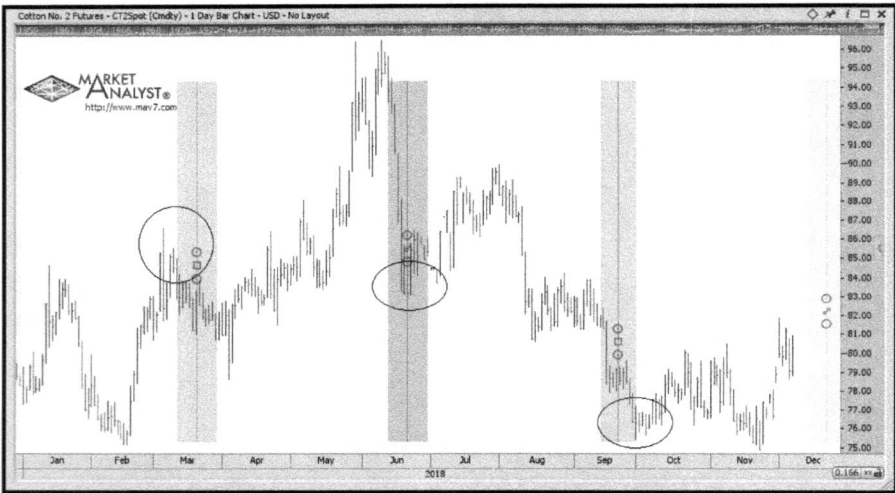

Figure 108   Cotton futures and Sun/natal Sun aspects

In 2019, transiting Sun will aspect natal Sun as follows:

Transiting Sun will pass 90 degrees to natal Sun from March 7 through March 23.

Transiting Sun will pass 0 degrees conjunct to natal Sun from June 10 through June 30.

Transiting Sun will pass 90 degrees to natal Sun from September 13 through September 30.

Transiting Sun will pass 180 degrees to natal Sun from December 12 through December 28.

One other astro phenomenon traders may wish to consider as a tool to use is the occurrence of Venus passing by the natal Moon position at 24 Pisces. Not a frequent event, it is nonetheless one to pay attention to. The price chart in Figure 109 illustrates. Note how the price high in May 2017 came right at a Venus/natal Moon transit. In 2018, a sharp rally in the February-March timeframe was stopped dead in its tracks at the transit of Venus past natal Moon. After the transit was complete, the rally resumed.

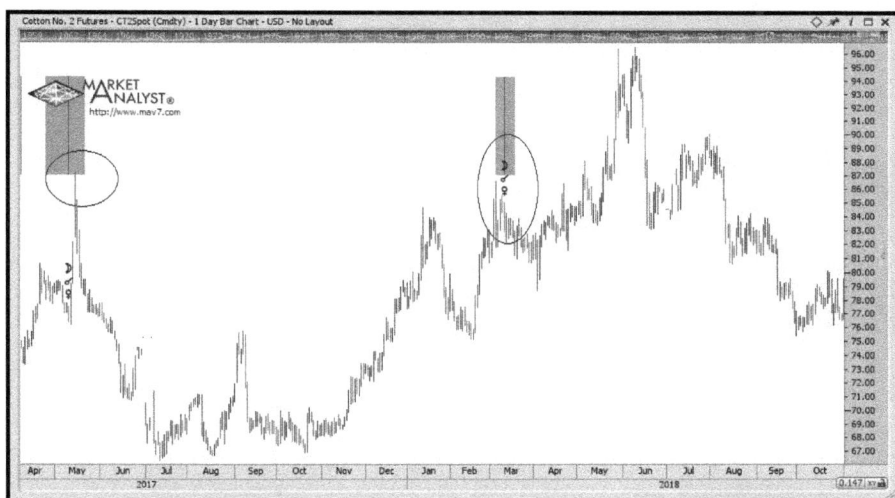

Figure 109 Cotton futures and Venus/natal Moon aspects

During 2019, Venus will transit past the natal Moon during mid-April.

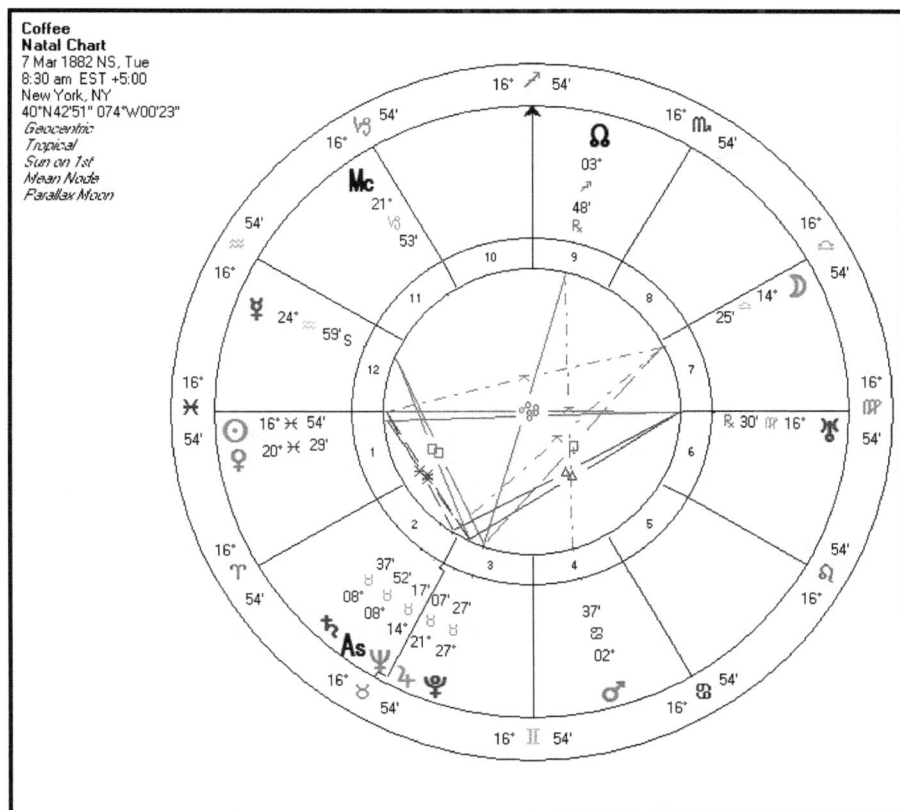

Figure 110 Coffee futures First Trade horoscope

Coffee futures started trading in New York in early March of 1882. The horoscope wheel in Figure 110 illustrates planetary placements at that time.

Natal Transits

In the Coffee horoscope, note the 180 degree aspect between Sun and Uranus. Louise McWhirter in her 1937 writings cautioned it is not wise to invest in situations where this sort of aspect exists because one will experience many wild ups and downs in price over time. A quick look at a 10 year price chart of Coffee reveals a price range of $0.65/pound to $3.06/pound with many wild swings. Point taken Ms. McWhirter.

The Coffee price chart in Figure 111 has been overlaid with events of transiting Sun making 0, 90 and 180 degree aspects to the natal Sun position at 16 Pisces.

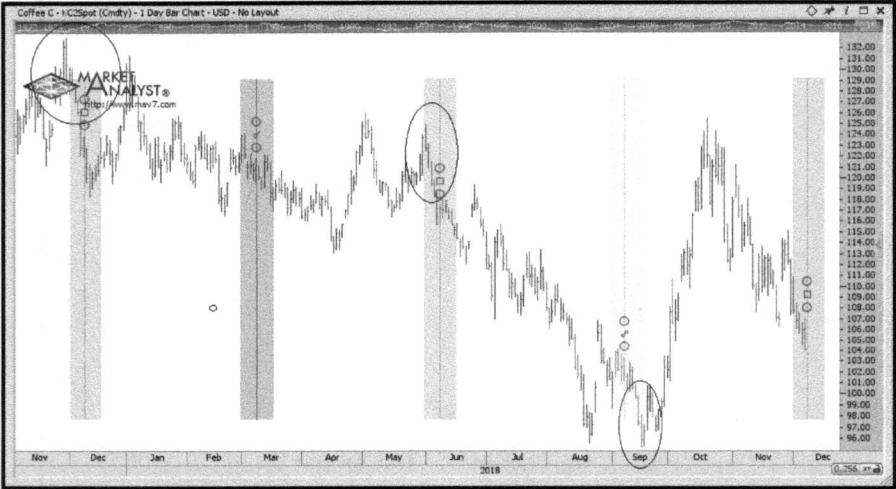

Figure 111 Coffee prices and natal transits

In 2019, transiting Sun will aspect natal Sun as follows:

Transiting Sun will pass 0 degrees conjunct to natal Sun from February 29 through March 16.

Transiting Sun will pass 90 degrees conjunct to natal Sun from May 31 through June 17.

Transiting Sun will pass 180 degrees to natal Sun from August 31 through September 19.

Transiting Sun will pass 90 degrees to natal Sun from December 10 through December 16.

non-Natal Transits

The positioning of Sun opposite Uranus in the 1882 natal horoscope is intrigiung. It turns out that real time aspects between Sun and Uranus can be used to further assist the Coffee trader with decision making. I am particularly drawn to the Sun 180 degree opposition aspects to Uranus. An aspect in 2016 came just shy of a significant price peak. A similar aspect in 2015 saw Coffee rally from 114 cents/pound to 137 cents per pound and then collapse. The same aspect in 2014 saw Coffee peak at 225 cents per pound and then erode all the way down to 112 cents per pound over the ensuing 11 months. These opposition events between Sun and Uranus will sometimes fall just shy of the actual price turning point, but they do seem to be ominous nonetheless. Figure 112 illustrates further. Notice that in 2018 a key reversal in early May came mere days after a conjunction event and another reversal came in October at an opposition event.

Figure 112 Coffee prices and Sun/Uranus aspects

For 2018, Sun will make the following hard aspects (0,90, 180 degree) with Uranus:

90 degrees from mid to late January.

0 degrees from mid to late April.

90 degrees from late July through August 10.

180 degrees from late October through November 3.

Sugar

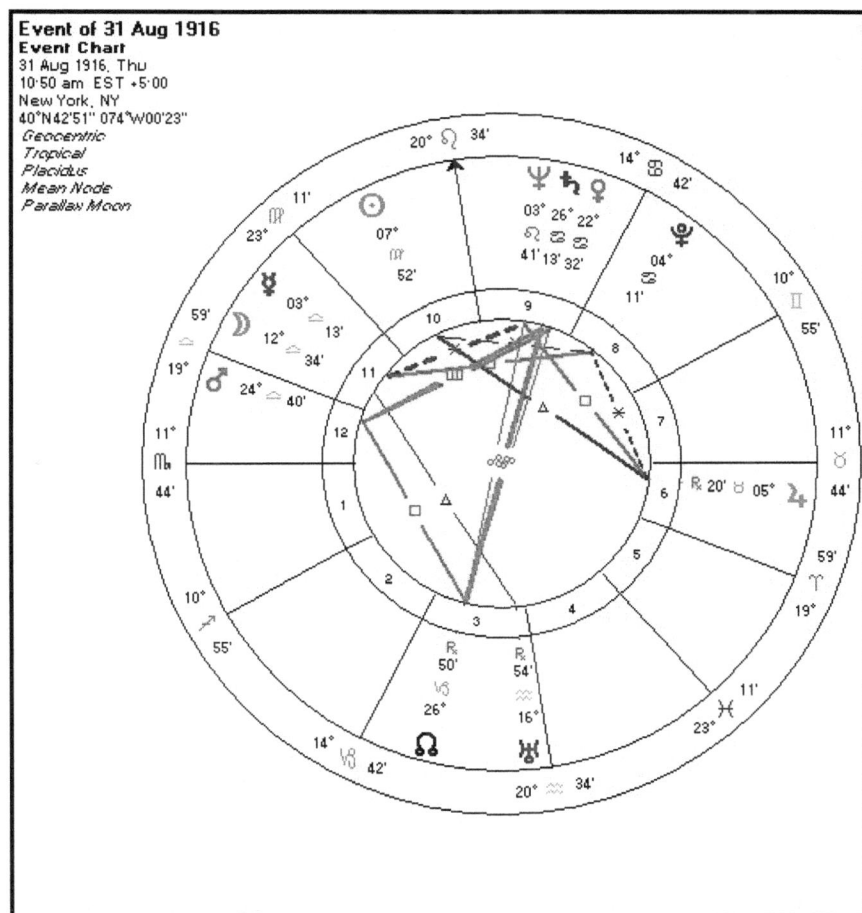

Figure 113 Sugar Futures First Trade horoscope

Sugar as a bulk commodity started trading in New York as early as 1881. My combing through old editions of New York newspapers suggests that in September 1914 there were plans to open a formal Sugar Exchange, but these plans were scuttled by World War 1. I am led to understand that a formal Exchange did open on August 31, 1916. The horoscope wheel in Figure 113 illustrates planetary placements at that time. What stands out on this chart wheel is the T-Square formation with Mars at its apex.

Natal Transits

Events of transiting Sun making 0, 90 and 180 degree aspects to the natal Mars location at 24 Libra have a high propensity to align to pivot swing points. The price chart in Figure 114 illustrates further. A significant price peak and reversal in January 2018 came days ahead of a square aspect. A conjunct aspect in October, 2018 delivered another price peak and reversal.

Figure 114 Sugar prices and natal transits

For 2019, transiting Sun will make the following aspects to natal Mars:

90 degrees from January 8 through the 23rd

180 degrees from April 6 through the 23rd

90 degrees from July 9 through the 25th

0 degrees from October 10 through the 26th

Retrograde

Mercury retrograde events have a propensity to align to short term trend changes on Sugar price as the chart in Figure 115 illustrates. Keep your eye on Mercury retrograde events and Sugar trends.

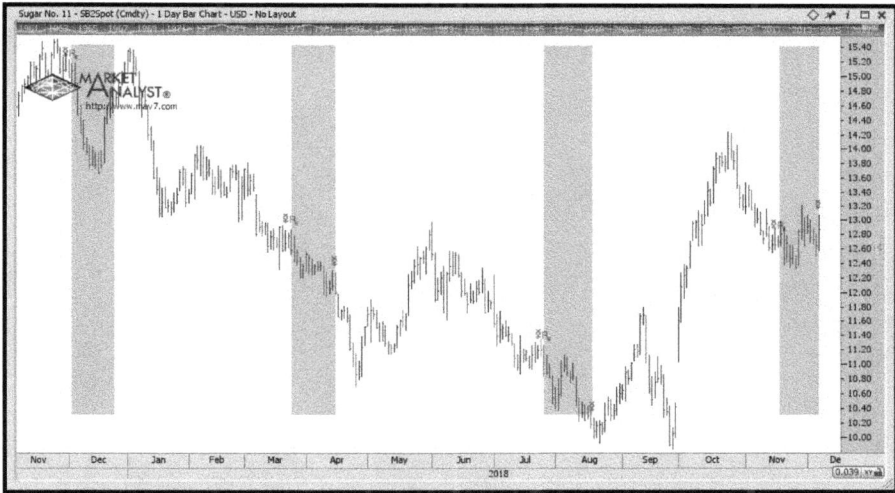

Figure 115 Mercury retrograde and Sugar price

For 2019, Mercury will be:

> ➢ In retrograde from March 5 through March 27.

> ➢ In retrograde from July 7 through July 31.

> ➢ In retrograde from October 31 through November 19.

Cocoa

Cocoa futures started trading in New York in early October 1925. The horoscope wheel in Figure 116 illustrates planetary placements at that time.

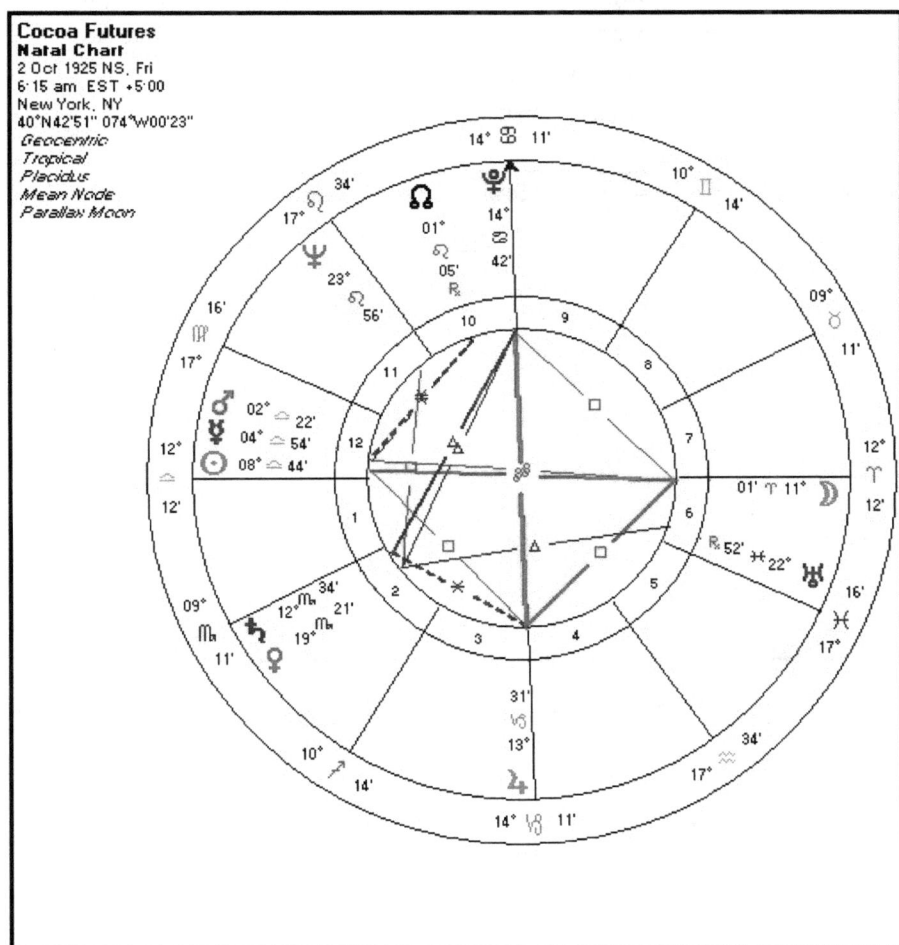

Figure 116 Cocoa futures First Trade horoscope

What I find peculiar on this horoscope wheel is the Mid-Heaven point is located at 14 of Cancer, that same mysterious point that appears in the First Trade horoscope of the New York Stock Exchange.

Retrograde

Mercury retrograde events have a high propensity to align to pivot swing points on Cocoa price. The price chart in Figure 117 illustrates further. Sometimes a Mercury retrograde event can deliver some erratic volatility as part of an ongoing trend, while other times the retrograde event can bring about a complete change of trend either immediately before the retrograde or immediately after. Either way, Mercury retrograde events deserve close scrutiny.

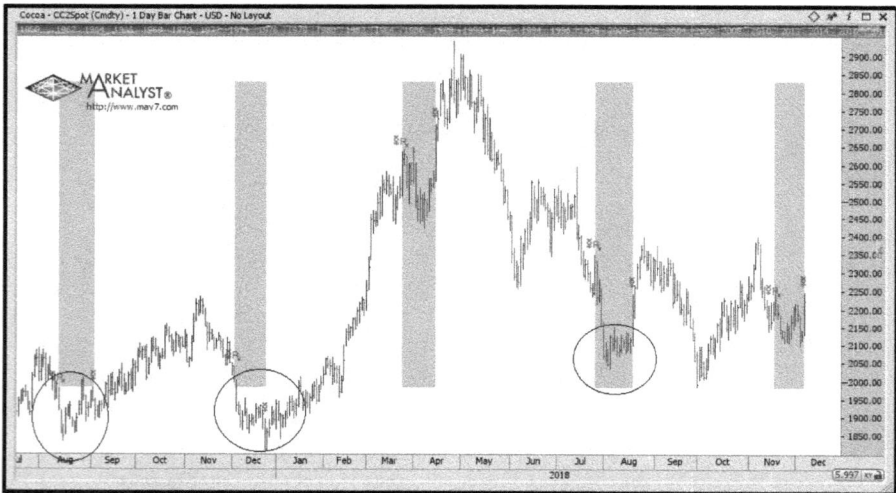

Figure 117 Mercury retrograde and Cocoa price

For 2019, Mercury will be:

> ➤ In retrograde from March 5 through March 27.

> ➤ In retrograde from July 7 through July 31.

> ➤ In retrograde from October 31 through November 19.

Conjunctions and Elongations

The 1925 natal horoscope shows Sun and Mercury conjunct (0 degrees apart). My research has shown that events of Mercury being at its maximum easterly and westerly elongations and events of Mercury being at its Inferior and Superior conjunctions align quite well to pivot swing points. The price chart in Figure 118 illustrates both phenomena further. I am particularly intrigued with the East and west elongation alignment to pivot price points.

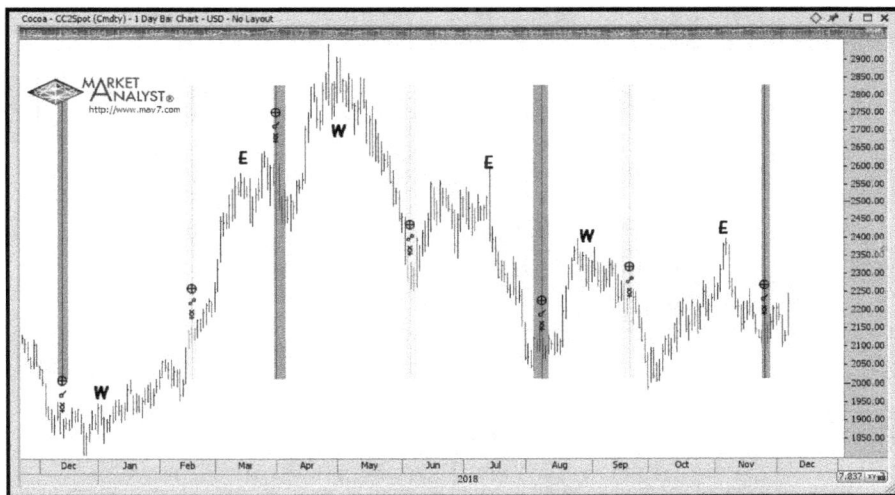

Figure 118 Cocoa price and Mercury cycles

For 2019, Mercury will be at its greatest easterly elongation February 27, June 23 and October 23. Greatest westerly elongations will occur at April 11, August 9, November 28.

For 2019, Mercury will be at Inferior Conjunction March 15, July 21, and November 4. Superior Conjunctions will occur January 30, May 21, and September 4.

Summary

This chapter has covered a great deal of ground. To help you frame all the contained information, the following data summary has been prepared. For each month, simply turn to that part of this chapter that deals with the stated commodity and review the astrological event(s) that will impact the commodity.

Month	Commodity
January	Silver, Gold, Euro, Aussie Dollar, 30 Year Bonds, 10 Year Treasuries, Coffee, Sugar, Cocoa,
February	Gold, Coffee, Aussie Dollar, Canadian Dollar
March	Gold, Silver, 30 Year Bonds, 10 Year Treasuries, Euro, Canadian Dollar, Cotton, Cocoa, Copper,
April	Cocoa, Aussie Dollar, Sugar, Coffee, Crude Oil, 10 Year Treasuries
May	Canadian Dollar, Silver, Coffee
June	Silver, Gold, Euro, Canadian Dollar, 30 Year Bonds, 10 Year Treasuries, Cotton, Crude Oil,
July	Coffee, Soybeans, Gold, Canadian Dollar, Cocoa, Sugar, Copper, Wheat, Aussie Dollar, 10
August	Cocoa, Canadian Dollar, Aussie Dollar, Wheat, Soybeans, Coffee
September	Gold, Silver, Canadian Dollar, Aussie Dollar, Euro, Cotton, Soybeans. Wheat, 30 Year Bonds
October	Silver, 10 Year Treasuries, Sugar, Coffee, Crude Oil, Aussie Dollar, Soybeans
November	Gold, Cocoa, Sugar, Soybeans, Wheat, Copper, 10 Year Treasuries, Aussie Dollar, Canadian
December	Gold, Canadian Dollar, 10 Year Treasuries, 30 Year Bonds, cocoa, Coffee, Cotton, Crude Oil,

12

Lines Across Time

Gann Fan Lines

Gann lines are a technique in which a starting point of a significant high or low is selected. From this point, angles (vectors) are projected outwards. These vectors are the 1x1, 1x2, 1x4, 1x8 and the 2x1, 4x1 and 8x1. In and of themselves, these Gann Lines are not related to Astrology. However, in my opinion, they should be applied to charts and used in combination with Astrology.

Many market data software platforms will come with a Gann Fan function already built in. The confusion with Gann lines comes from the mathematical method of constructing the lines. In fact, in the Market Analyst program there are no fewer than ten ways to apply Gann Lines to a chart. If Mr. Gann were around today he would probably shake his head in bewilderment at how convoluted his technique has become. My preference for apply Gann Lines is the methodology used by Daniel Ferrera in his book *Gann for the Active Trader*. Ferrera's method is based on the Gann Square of Nine mathematics.

To illustrate the creation of Gann lines, I will use a standard example of Gold prices and this example appears in past Almanacs. Follow the methodology that is described in the following paragraphs and you will soon have Gann Lines on your chart. You do not need a fancy software program to do this. The methodology is as follows:

On March 17, 2014, Gold made a price high at $1392. This is the point from which I wish to extend Gann lines.

Step 1: Take the $1392 and express it simply as the number 1392. Take the square root of the number 1392 and you get 37.3. This will be your time factor.

Step 2: Subtract 1 from 37.3 and re-square this figure to get 1318.

Step 3: We can now state that our time factor is 37.3 calendar days. For simplicity, we can round this off to 37 days. We can further state that our price factor is 1392 minus 1318 = $74.

Step 4: From the March 17 date, extend a line so that it passes through the time co-ordinate (March 17+37 days = April 23) and the price co-ordinate $1318. This line is the Gann 1x1 line.

Step 5: From the March 17 date, extend a line so that it passes through the time co-ordinate (March 17+(37 x 2) days = May 30) and the price co-ordinate $1318. This line is the Gann 1x2 line.

Step 6: From the March 17 date, extend a line so that it passes through the time co-ordinate ((March 17+(0.5)*37)days = April 4) and the price co-ordinate $1318. This line is the Gann 2x1 line.

Step 7: From the March 17 date, extend a line so that it passes through the time co-ordinate ((March 17+(0.25)*37)days = March 26) and the price co-ordinate $1318. This line is the Gann 4x1 line.

The Gold price chart in Figure 119 has these Gann lines overlaid starting from the March $1392 high. This chart has been prepared in the Market Analyst software platform, but as I say you do not necessarily need a fancy software program. A pencil and a ruler could be used to draw lines onto a chart printout.

Figure 119 Gann Lines applied to a Gold Chart

Notice from the $1392 high, price action dropped, following the 4x1 line. A rally then pushed price up to the 1x1 line. The rally failed and price fell back to the 2x1 line. A sideways consolidation then ensued for several weeks. A price low was registered right at the 1x1 line. Price then rallied up through the 1x2 line and hit resistance at the 1x4 line. Price then drifted lower and eventually recorded a significant low in the November 2014 timeframe just a bit underneath the 1x2 line. In early 2015, a rally failed just shy of the 1x8 line. It is fascinating how these Lines act as support and resistance.

To bring matters into the current timeframe, Figure 120 presents a Gold chart with Gann Lines applied from a July 6, 2016 high that remains unchallenged as of this time of writing. Figure 120 also has Gann Lines applied to the significant price lows that were recorded in late 2016.

The downward sloping 1x8 line provided support in late 2017 and again in August 2018. The upward sloping 1x4 line is providing resistance to a rally in February 2018. Now, use this Gann Line chart in combination with the astrological events affecting Gold outlined in the previous chapter and you have a powerful tool at your hands.

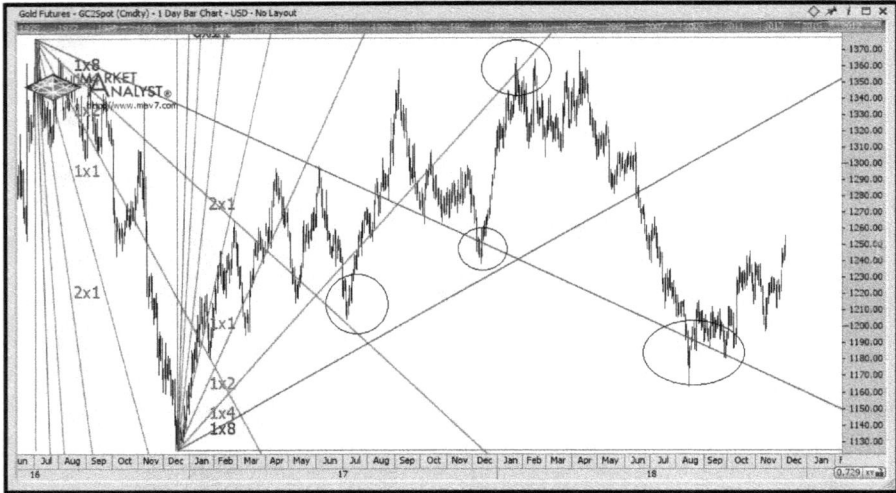

Figure 120 Gann Lines and Gold 2018

To assist you further, I have applied Gann lines to the price high point made in early 2018. This is illustrated in Figure 121.

Figure 121 Gann Lines and Gold 2019

Let's take a look at one more standard example which appears in past Almanacs. Consider the price action of Crude Oil which registered a significant high on June 20, 2014 at $107.73.

Step 1: Take the $107.73 and express it simply as the number 1077.3. Take the square root of the number 1077.3 and you get 32.8. This will be your time factor.

Step 2: Subtract 1 from 32.8 and re-square this figure to get 1011.24.

Step 3: We can now state that our time factor is 33 calendar days. We can further state that our price factor is 1077 minus 1011 = $66.

Step 4: From the June 20 date, you will extend a line so that it passes through the time co-ordinate (June 20 +33 days = July 24) and the price co-ordinate $101.1. This line is the Gann 1x1 line.

Step 5: From the June 20 date, you will extend a line so that it passes through the time co-ordinate (June 20+(33 x 2) days = August 26) and the price co-ordinate $101.1. This line is the Gann 1x2 line.

Next, consider that Crude Oil made a significant low on March 18, 2015 at the $42.30 level.

Step 1: Take the $42.30 level and express it simply as the number 423.0. Take the square root of the number 423.0 and you get 20.56. This will be your time factor.

Step 2: Add 1 to 20.56 and re-square this figure to get 464.83.

Step 3: We can now state that our time factor is 20.56 calendar days. We can further state that our price factor is 464 minus 423 = $41.

Step 4: From the March 18 date, you will extend a line so that it passes through the time co-ordinate (March 18 +20 days = April 8) and the price co-ordinate $46.48. This line is the Gann 1x1 line.

Step 5: From the March 18 date, you will extend a line so that it passes through the time co-ordinate (March 18 + (20 x 2) days = April 28) and the price co-ordinate $46.48. This line is the Gann 1x2 line.

Step 6: From the March 18 date, you will extend a line so that it passes through the time co-ordinate (March 18 + (20 x 8) days = August 29) and the price co-ordinate $46.48. This line is the Gann 1x8 line.

The Crude Oil price chart in Figure 122 has these Gann lines overlaid starting from the June 2014 $107.73 high.

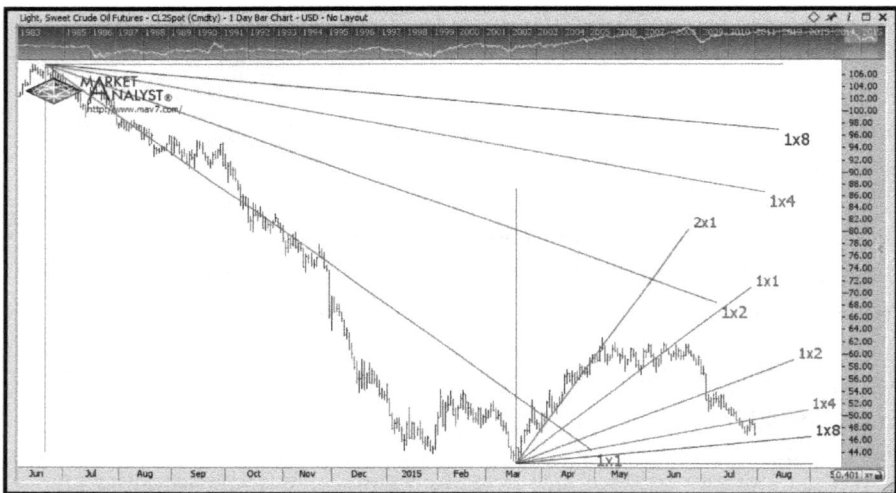

Figure 122   Gann Lines applied to a Crude Oil chart

To bring this Oil example into the current timeframe, recall that Crude made a significant low on February 11, 2016. Another low was made in August of 2016 at the $40 mark. Another low at $42 was made in June 2017. Using this 2017 low, Figure 123 presents a crude Oil price chart overlaid with Gann Lines. Note that the recent lows in December 2018 have taken out the 1x8 line. Once some stability is recognized at these levels, Gann lines can then be projected forwards in time for 2019.

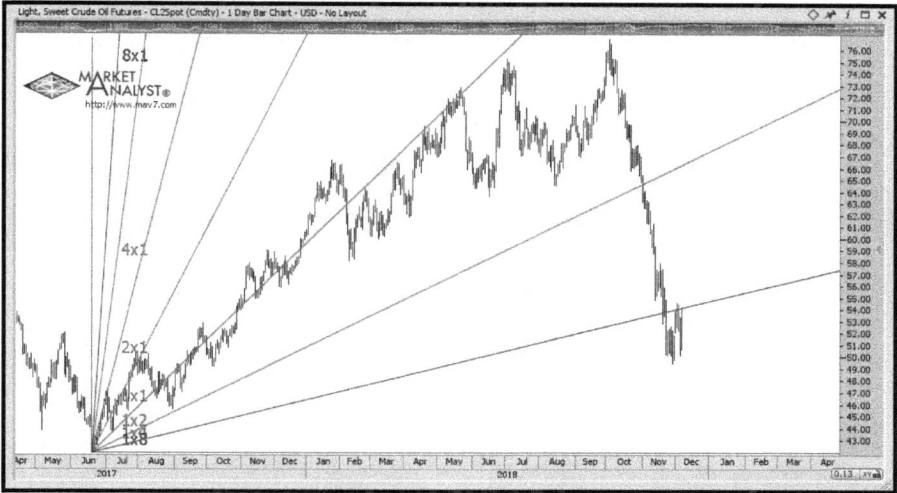

Figure 123 Updated Gann Lines and Crude Oil

Gann Planetary Transit Lines

While on the subject of Gann and Lines, there is one astrological technique whose power continues to amaze me. The technique I refer to is Gann Planetary Transit Lines. (For a detailed description of how to construct Transit Lines, see my second book, *The Lost Science* or see Jeanne Long's book, *The Universal Clock*. The construction methodology is quite simple and either of these publications will step you through it).

Transit lines involve taking the longitudinal position of a given planet and converting that longitude to price by means of the Wheel of 24 (also known as the Universal Clock). Typically, transit lines are plotted for Mars, Jupiter, Saturn, Uranus and Neptune. Once the transit lines have been calculated and plotted, one can then overlay price data on the chart.

Figure 124 illustrates a chart of Crude Oil prices to which I have added the Uranus transit lines. This chart has been prepared in the Market Analyst software platform using the built-in Gann Planetary Transit function. Notice how price highs in each of 2012, 2013, 2014 and 2015 came in very close conjunction to one of the Uranus transit lines. Early

2016 saw Crude make a significant low at near $26 per barrel, which conveniently enough aligned to a Uranus transit line. As I craft this part of the manuscript in December 2018, Crude Oil is again acting weak. Figure 125 illustrates. Support appears to exist at the $48 level.

Figure 124 Crude Oil and Uranus Transit Lines

Figure 125 Crude Oil and Uranus Transit Lines 2018

To further illustrate the power of transit lines, consider the chart in Figure 126 of the Dow Jones Industrial Average which has been overlaid with Mars transit lines. Note how these transit lines have frequently aligned to support and resistance levels. More importantly, note how in 2017 Dow Jones price action has been tightly constrained by two Mars lines.

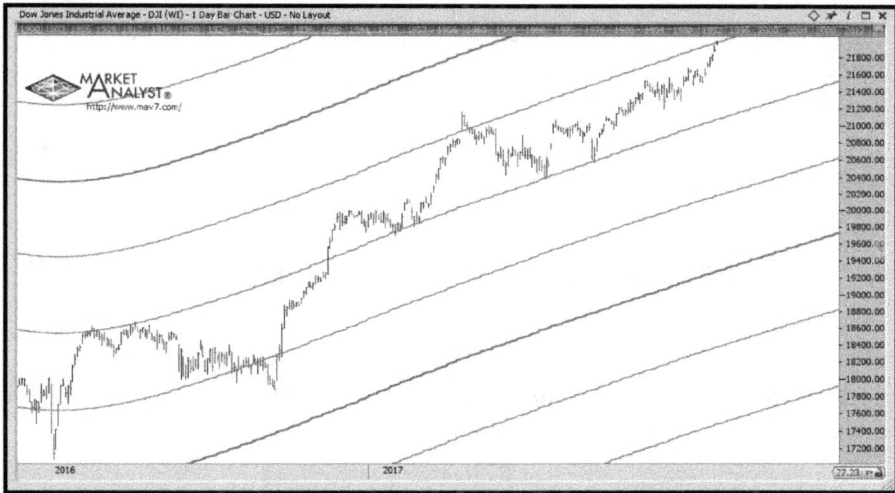

Figure 126 Dow Jones Average and Mars Transit Lines

Figure 127 brings matters up to date. The Mars lines continue to act as support and resistance.

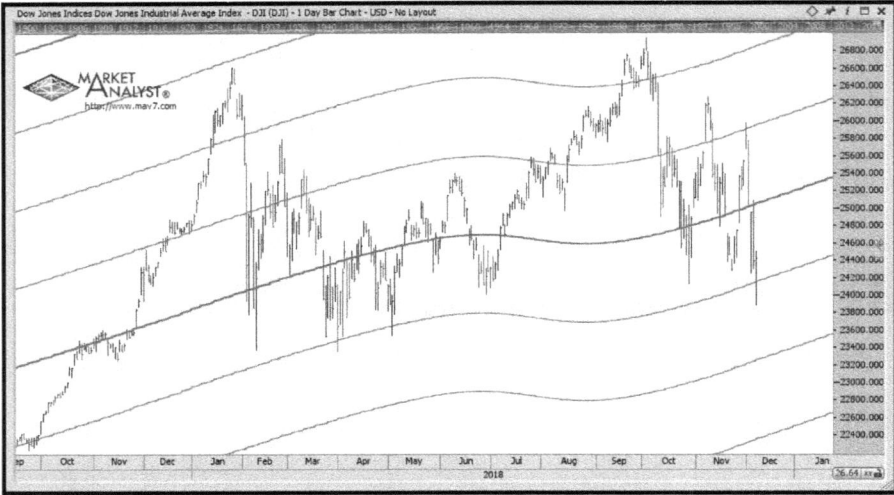

Figure 127 Dow Jones and Mars Transit Lines 2018

For readers in Australia, Figure 128 illustrates how the various harmonics of Jupiter transit lines offer support and resistance to the S&P/ASX 200.

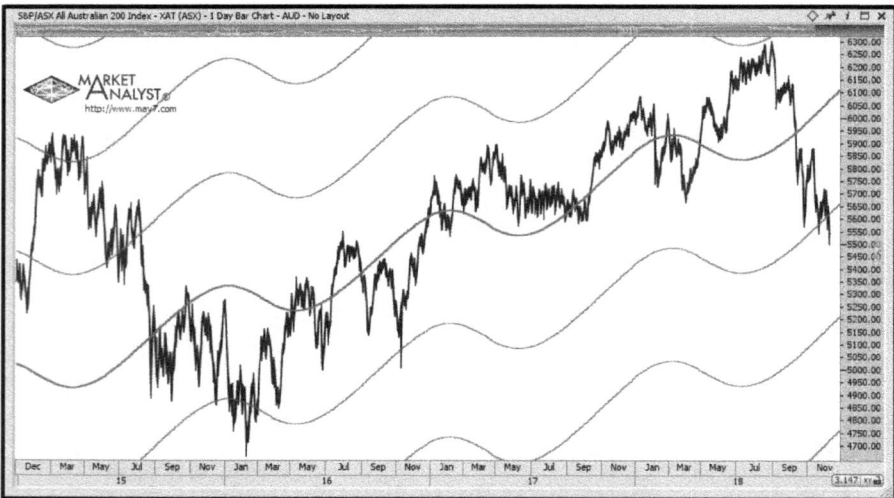

Figure 128 ASX 200 and Jupiter Transit Lines 2018

Newton and Einstein

In the early 1700s and scientist Sir Isaac Newton developed his theory of Universal Gravitation in which he said planets in our solar system are attracted to one another by gravity. Newton further said that space and time were absolute and that the world functioned according to an absolute order. Furthermore, he said that space was a three-dimensional entity and time was a two-dimensional entity.

In the early 1900's, Albert Einstein advanced his Theory of Relativity that posited Newton's absolute model was outdated. Einstein said the passage of time of an object was related to its speed with respect to that of another observer. Thus was penned the concept of relative space-time in which space was not uniform.

Einstein further stated that relative space-time could be distorted depending on the density of matter. That is, space-time in the area of the Sun is more distorted because the Sun has a great, huge mass. Light particles travelling near the Sun are then distorted from their linear path due to the mass of the Sun.

Quantum Price Lines

Quantum Price Lines are based on this quantum theory. The whole notion of Quantum Lines posits that the price of a stock, index or commodity can be thought of as a light particle or electron that can occupy different energy levels or orbital shells.

Author and market researcher Fabio Oreste has done a masterful job of taking quantum physics, blending it with the curvature mathematics of Riemann and applying the whole thing to price charting. Price is considered to be akin to light particles. These light particles are then deflected by actions of planets. This deflection is what gives us price highs and lows on a chart. Essentially, what Oreste has done is take the Gann Transit Line notion and marry it to modern physics and bring it into the 21st century. Oreste's book is entitled *Quantum Trading* and is available through most on-line book-sellers.

To save you the trouble of buying the book, the Oreste formula for Quantum Price Line calculation is :

Quantum Line = (N x 360) + PSO ;

Where PSO = heliocentric planetary longitude **x** Conversion Scale
Where N= the harmonic level = 2^n ; 1,2,4,8,16 ….
Where Conversion Scale = 2^n ; 1,2,4,8,16 ….

When dealing with prices less than 360, the inverse variation of the formula is used.

Quantum Line = (1/N x 360) + PSO

The technique then allows one to calculate various sub-divisions of these Quantum Lines. Taking the value of the calculated Quantum Line, one would generate the sub-divisions by multiplying by 1.0625, 1.125, 1.875, 1.25 etc… in steps of 0.0625.

Please note the use of heliocentric planetary data in these Quantum Line calculations. There are websites that will provide you with this data. One site I use is found at: www.astro.com/swisseph. Alternatively, you can find a Heliocentric Ephemeris book. The one that I have is entitled: *The American Heliocentric Ephemeris, 2001-2050.* I managed to find it at a bookstore in London, UK.

To go into a lengthy description of Quantum Lines would quickly double the size of this manuscript. In the interest of brevity, what follows is a listing of the Quantum lines you may wish to overlay onto your various charts for 2019. You may be shocked to find how price action tends to closely respect these Lines and sub-divisions thereof.

S&P 500 Index

I have found that the **Pluto** quantum lines and **Neptune** Quantum Lines (Conversion Scale =2, N=2) work quite well for the S&P 500 Index. During 2019, consider drawing the following suite of Quantum Lines onto your daily chart of the S&P500 Index. Each line should start at January 1, 2019 and terminate at December 31, 2019.

Pluto - January 2019	Pluto - December 2019
1706	1711
1787	1793
1868	1874
1950	1956
2031	2037
2112	2119
2193	2200
2275	2282
2356	2363
2437	2445
2518	2526
2600	2608
2762	2771
2925	2934
3087	3097

Neptune - January 2019	Neptune - December 2019
1674	1679
1762	1767
1850	1855
1938	1944
2026	2032
2115	2121
2203	2209
2291	2297
2379	2386
2467	2474
2555	2562
2643	2651
2731	2739
2820	2828
2996	3004
3172	3181

Nasdaq Composite Index

I have found that the **Pluto** quantum lines (Conversion Scale =4, N=8) work quite well for the Nasdaq Composite. During 2019, consider drawing the following suite of Quantum Lines onto your daily chart of the Nasdaq Composite. Each line should start at January 1, 2019 and terminate at December 31, 2019.

.

January 2019	December 2019
5302	5313
5555	5566
5807	5819
6060	6072
6312	6325
6565	6578
6817	6831
7070	7084
7322	7337
7575	7590
7827	7843
8080	8096

Dow Jones Industrial Average

I have found that the **Pluto** quantum lines (Conversion Scale =2, N=32) work quite well for the Dow Jones Average. During 2019, consider drawing the following suite of Quantum Lines onto your daily chart of the Dow. Each line should start at January 1, 2019 and terminate at December 31, 2019.

January 2019	December 2019
19020	19032
19812	19825
20605	20618
21397	21411
22190	22204
22982	22997
23775	23790
24567	24583
25360	25376
25712	25721
27225	27234
28737	28747
30250	30260
31762	31773

FTSE 100 Index

I have found that the **Pluto** Quantum Lines (Conversion Scale =8, N=2) work quite well for the FTSE 100. During 2019, consider drawing the following suite of Quantum Lines onto your daily chart of the FTSE. Each line should start at January 1, 2019 and terminate at December 31, 2019.

.

January 2019	December 2019
5130	5157
5320	5348
5510	5539
5700	5730
5890	5921
6080	6112
6460	6494
6840	6876
7220	7258
7600	7640
7980	8022
8360	8404

German DAX Index

I have found that the **Pluto** Quantum Lines (Conversion Scale=16, N=2) work quite well for the DAX. During 2019, consider drawing the following suite of Quantum Lines onto your daily chart of the DAX. Each line should start at January 1, 2019 and terminate at December 31, 2019.

January 2019	December 2019
8040	8088
8375	8425
8710	8762
9045	9099
9380	9773
10050	10110
10385	10447
10625	10693
11250	11322
11875	11951
12500	12580
13125	13209
13750	13838
14375	14467

Gold Futures

I have found that the **Pluto** Quantum Lines (Conversion Scale=1, N=2) work quite well for Gold. During 2019, consider drawing the following suite of Quantum Lines onto your daily chart of Gold. Each line should start at January 1, 2019 and terminate at December 31, 2019.

.

January 2019	December 2019
1073	1075
1136	1138
1199	1201
1262	1265
1325	1328
1388	1391
1451	1454
1515	1518
1578	1581
1641	1644
1704	1707
1767	1771
1830	1834
1893	1897
1956	1960

Silver Futures

I have found that the **Pluto** Quantum Lines (Conversion Scale=1/64 and 1/32, N=1/64 and 1/32) work quite well for Silver. During 2019, consider drawing the following suite of Quantum Lines onto your daily chart of Silver. Each line should start at January 1, 2019 and terminate at December 31, 2019.

January 2019	December 2019
13.33	13.37
13.96	14.00
14.60	14.64
15.23	15.28
15.86	15.91
16.50	16.55
17.13	17.19
17.77	17.82
18.40	18.46
19.04	19.10
19.67	19.73

Currency Futures (Canadian Dollar, Australian Dollar, Japanese Yen)

I have found that the **Pluto** Quantum Lines (Conversion Scale=1/1024, N=1/1024) work quite well for these currencies. During 2019, consider drawing the following suite of Quantum Lines onto your daily chart of each of these currencies. Each line should start at January 1, 2019 and terminate at December 31, 2019.

January 2019	December 2019
0.6370	0.6390
0.6768	0.6789
0.7166	0.7188
0.7564	0.7588
0.7963	0.7987
0.8361	0.8386
0.8759	0.8786
0.9157	0.9185
0.9953	0.9984
1.0351	1.0383
1.0749	1.0782
1.1148	1.1182
1.1546	1.1581
1.1944	1.1981
1.2342	1.2380
1.2740	1.2780

Currency Futures (Euro and British Pound)

I have found that the **Pluto** Quantum Lines (Conversion Scale=1/1024 & 1/512, N=1/1024 & 1/512) work quite well for these currencies. During 2019, consider drawing the following suite of Quantum Lines onto your daily chart of each of these currencies. Each line should start at January 1, 2019 and terminate at December 31, 2019.

January 2019	December 2019
1.0351	1.0383
1.0749	1.0782
1.1148	1.1182
1.1546	1.1581
1.1944	1.1981
1.2342	1.2380
1.2740	1.2780
1.3487	1.3529
1.4281	1.4325
1.5075	1.5121
1.5868	1.5917
1.6662	1.6713
1.7455	1.7509
1.8284	1.8304
1.9042	1.9100

Wheat and Corn Futures

I have found that the **Pluto** Quantum Lines (Conversion Scale=1/256 & 1/128, N=1/256 & 1/128) work quite well for these currencies. During 2019, consider drawing the following suite of Quantum Lines onto your daily chart of each of these grains. Each line should start at January 1, 2019 and terminate at December 31, 2019.

January 2019	December 2019
3.96	3.97
4.12	4.13
4.28	4.29
4.44	4.45
4.60	4.61
4.76	4.77
4.91	4.93
5.07	5.09
5.39	5.41
5.71	5.73
6.03	6.05
6.34	6.36
6.66	6.68
6.98	7.00
7.30	7.32
7.61	7.64

Soybean Futures

I have found that the **Pluto** Quantum Lines (Conversion Scale=1/64 & 1/128, N=1/64 & 1/128) work quite well for Beans. During 2019, consider drawing the following suite of Quantum Lines onto your daily chart of Beans. Each line should start at January 1, 2019 and terminate at December 31, 2019.

January 2019	December 2019
8.56	8.59
8.88	8.91
9.20	9.23
9.52	9.55
9.83	9.86
10.15	10.18
10.79	10.82
11.42	11.46
12.06	12.09
12.69	12.73
13.33	13.37
13.96	14.00
14.60	14.64

Crude Oil Futures

I have found that the **Pluto** Quantum Lines (Conversion Scale=1/32, 1/16 N=1/32, 1/16) work quite well for Oil. During 2019, consider drawing the following suite of Quantum Lines onto your daily chart of Oil. Each line should start at January 1, 2019 and terminate at December 31, 2019.

January 2019	December 2019
26.66	26.70
27.93	27.97
29.20	29.24
30.47	30.51
31.74	31.78
33.00	33.06
34.27	34.33
35.54	35.60
36.81	36.87
38.08	38.14
39.35	39.41
40.62	40.75
43.16	43.29
45.70	45.84
48.24	48.39
50.78	50.93

53.32	53.48
55.85	56.03
58.40	58.57
60.93	61.12
63.47	63.67
66.01	66.21
68.55	68.76

The Script Tool function in Market Analyst works exceptionally well for creating Quantum Price lines to overlay onto price charts. To take your financial market astrology to the next level, consider taking out a trial subscription to Market Analyst software. Paste the following link into your browser:

http://www.mav8.com/investingsuccess

30 Year Bond Futures

I have found that the **Saturn** Quantum Lines (Conversion Scale=1/4 & 1/8, N=1/4 & 1/8) work fairly well for Bonds. During 2019, consider drawing the following suite of Quantum Lines onto your daily chart of Bonds. Each line should start at January 1, 2019 and terminate at December 31, 2019.

January 2019	December 2019
100	101
105	106
110	111
115	116
120	122
125	127
130	132
135	137
140	142
145	147
150	152
155	157

10 Year Treasury Note Futures

I have found that the **Pluto** Quantum Lines (Conversion Scale=1/8, N=1/8) work not too badly for Treasuries. During 2019, consider drawing the following suite of Quantum Lines onto your daily chart of Treasuries. Each line should start at January 1, 2019 and terminate at December 31, 2019.

January 2019	December 2019
106.64	106.96
111.71	112.06
116.79	117.15
121.87	122.25
126.95	127.34
132.03	132.43
137.10	137.53

Sugar Futures

I have found that the **Pluto** quantum lines (Conversion Scale = 1/64 and 1/32). During 2019, consider drawing the following suite of quantum lines onto your daily chart of Sugar prices. Each line should start at January 1, 2019 and terminate at December 31, 2019.

January 2019	December 2019
10.15	10.18
10.79	10.82
11.42	11.46
12.06	12.09
12.69	12.73
13.33	13.37
13.96	14.00
14.60	14.64
15.23	15.28
15.86	15.91
16.50	16.55
17.13	17.19
17.77	17.82
18.35	18.37
18.98	19.01
19.61	19.64

Cocoa Futures

I have found that the **Pluto** Quantum Lines (Conversion Scale=2 N=2) work quite well for Cocoa. During 2018, consider drawing the following suite of Quantum Lines onto your daily chart of Cocoa. Each line should start at January 1, 2018 and terminate at December 31, 2018.

January 2018	December 2018
1787	1793
1868	1874
1950	1956
2031	2037
2112	2119
2275	2282
2356	2363
2437	2445
2518	2526
2600	2771
2925	2934
3087	3097

13

Epilogue

I have taken you on a wide ranging journey in this Almanac to acquaint you with the mathematical and astrological links between investor emotion and market behavior. I sincerely hope you will embrace Financial Astrology as a valuable tool to assist you in your trading and investing activity. I hope you will pause often to reflect on the deeper connection between the financial markets, Astrology and the emotions of mankind. And, as unsettling as it may be, I further hope that you pause to reflect on the connection between Astrology and the men in dark suits who may be using it to manipulate the markets.

On that note, I will leave you with the words of Neil Turok from his 2012 book, *The Universe Within*.

"Perseverance leads to enlightenment. And the truth is more beautiful than your wildest dreams".

14

Glossary of Terms

Ascendant: One of four cardinal points on a horoscope, the Ascendant is situated in the East.

Aspect: The angular relationship between two planets measured in degrees.

Autumnal Equinox: (see Equinox) – That time of year when Sun is at 0 degrees Libra.

Conjunct: An angular relationship of 0 degrees between two planets.

Cosmo-biology: Changes in human emotion caused by changes in cosmic energy.

Descendant: One of four cardinal points on a horoscope, the Descendant is situated in the West.

Ephemeris: A daily tabular compilation of planetary and lunar positions.

Equinox: An event occurring twice annually, an equinox event marks the time when the tilt of the Earth's axis is neither toward or away from the Sun.

First Trade chart: A zodiac chart depicting the positions of the planets at the time a company's stock or a commodity future commenced trading on a recognized financial exchange.

First Trade date: The date a stock or commodity futures contract first began trading on a recognized exchange.

Full Moon: From a vantage point situated on Earth, when the Moon is seen to be 180 degrees to the Sun.

Geocentric Astrology: That version of Astrology in which the vantage point for determining planetary aspects is the Earth.

Heliocentric Astrology: That version of Astrology in which the vantage point for determining planetary aspects is the Sun.

House: A $1/12^{th}$ portion of the zodiac. Portions are not necessarily equal depending on the mathematical formula used to calculate the divisions.

Lunar Eclipse: A lunar eclipse occurs when the Sun, Earth, and Moon are aligned exactly, or very closely so, with the Earth in the middle. The Earth blocks the Sun's rays from striking the Moon.

Lunar Month: (see Synodic Month).

Lunation: (see New Moon).

Mid-Heaven: One of four cardinal points on a horoscope, the Mid-Heaven is situated in the South.

New Moon: From a vantage point situated on Earth, when the Moon is seen to be 0 degrees to the Sun.

North Node of Moon: The intersection points between the Moon's plane and Earth's ecliptic are termed the North and South nodes. Astrologers tend to focus on the North node and Ephemeris tables clearly list the zodiacal position of the North Node for each calendar day.

Orb: The amount of flexibility or tolerance given to an aspect.

Retrograde motion: The apparent backwards motion of a planet through the zodiac signs when viewed from a vantage point on Earth.

Sidereal Month: The Moon orbits Earth with a slightly elliptical pattern in approximately 27.3 days, relative to a fixed frame of reference.

Sidereal Orbital Period: The time required for a planet to make one full orbit of the Sun as viewed from a fixed vantage point on the Sun.

Siderograph: A mathematical equation developed by astrologer Donald Bradley in 1946 (By plotting the output of the equation against date, inflection points can be seen on the plotted curve. It is at these inflection points that human emotion is most apt to change resulting in a trend change on the Dow Jones or S&P 500 Index).

Solar Eclipse: A solar eclipse occurs when the Moon passes between the Sun and Earth and fully or partially blocks the Sun.

Solstice: Occurring twice annually, a solstice event marks the time when the Sun reaches its highest or lowest altitude above the horizon at noon.

Synodic Month: During a sidereal month (see Sidereal Month), Earth will revolve part way around the Sun thus making the average apparent time between one New Moon and the next New Moon longer than the sidereal month at approximately 29.5 days. This 29.5 day time span is called a Synodic Month or sometimes a Lunar Month.

Synodic Orbital Period: The time required for a planet to make one full orbit of the Sun as viewed from a fixed vantage point on Earth.

Vernal Equinox: That time of the year when Sun is at 0 degrees Aries.

Zodiac: An imaginary band encircling the 360 degrees of the planetary system divided into twelve equal portions of 30 degrees each.

Zodiac Wheel: A circular image broken into 12 portions of 30 degrees each. Each portion represents a different astrological sign.

15

Other Books By the Author

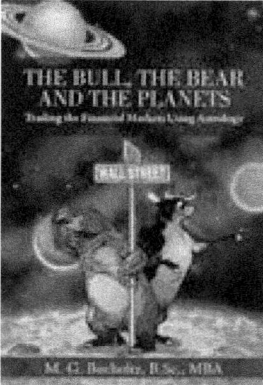

Once maligned by many, the subject of financial Astrology is now experiencing a revival as traders and investors seek deeper insight into the forces that move the financial markets.

The markets are a dynamic entity fueled by many factors, some of which we can easily comprehend, some of which are esoteric. This book introduces the reader to the notion that astrological phenomena can influence price action on financial markets and create trend changes across both short and longer term time horizons. From an introduction to the historical basics behind Astrology through to an examination of lunar Astrology and planetary aspects, the numerous illustrated examples in this book will introduce the reader the power of Astrology and its impact on both equity markets and commodity futures markets.

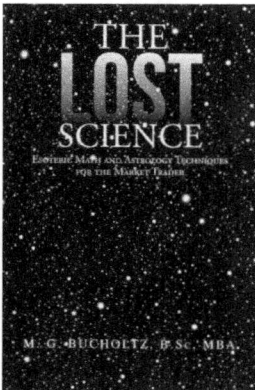

The financial markets are a reflection of the psychological emotions of traders and investors. These emotions ebb and flow in harmony with the forces of nature.

Scientific techniques and phenomena such as square root mathematics, the Golden Mean, the Golden Sequence, lunar events, planetary transits and planetary aspects have been used by civilizations dating as far back as the ancient Egyptians in order to comprehend the forces of nature.

The emotions of traders and investors can be seen to fluctuate in accordance with these forces of nature. Lunar events can be seen to align with trend changes on financial markets. Significant market cycles can be seen to align with planetary transits and aspects. Price patterns on stocks, commodity futures and market indices can be seen to conform to square root and Golden Mean mathematics.

In the early years of the 20th century the most successful traders on Wall Street, including the venerable W.D. Gann, used these scientific techniques and phenomena to profit from the markets. However, over the ensuing decades as technology has advanced, the science has been lost.

The Lost Science acquaints the reader with an extensive range of astrological and mathematical phenomena. From the Golden Mean and Fibonacci Sequence, to planetary transit lines and square roots through to an examination of lunar Astrology and planetary aspects, the numerous illustrated examples in this book will show the reader how these unique scientific phenomena impact the financial markets.

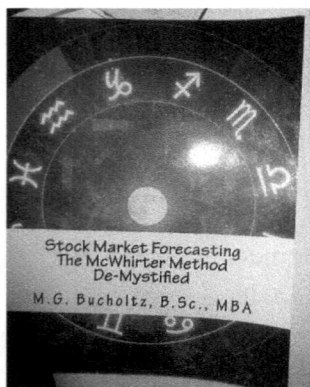

Stock Market Forecasting
The McWhirter Method
De-Mystified
M.G. Bucholtz, B.Sc., MBA

Very little is known about Louise McWhirter, except that in 1937 she wrote the book *McWhirter Theory of Stock Market Forecasting.*

In my travels to places as far away as the British Library in London, England to research financial Astrology, not once did I come across any other books by her. Not once did I find any other book from her era that even mentioned her name. All of this I find to be deeply mysterious. Whoever she was – she wrote only one book, and it was a powerful one that is as accurate today as it was back in 1937. The purpose of writing this book is suggested by the title itself – to de-mystify McWhirter's methodology - which is not exactly straightforward.

Can the movements of the Moon affect the stock market?

Are price swings on Crude Oil, Soybeans, the British pound and other financial instruments a reflection of planetary placements?

The answer to these questions is YES. Changes in price trends on the markets are in fact related to our changing emotions. Our emotions in turn are impacted by the changing events in our cosmos.

In the early part of the 20th century many successful traders on Wall Street, including the venerable W.D. Gann and the mysterious Louise McWhirter, understood that emotion was linked to the forces of the cosmos. They used astrological events and esoteric mathematics to predict changes in price trend and to profit from the markets.

However, in the latter part of the 20th century, the investment community has become more comfortable just relying on academic financial theory and the opinions of colorful television media personalities all wrapped up in a buy and hold mentality.

The Cosmic Clock has been written for traders and investors who are seeking to gain an understanding of the cosmic forces that influence emotion and the financial markets.

This book will acquaint you with an extensive range of astrological and mathematical phenomena. From the Golden Mean and Fibonacci Sequence through planetary transit lines, quantum lines, the McWhirter method, planetary conjunctions and market cycles. The numerous illustrated examples in this book will show you how these unique phenomena can deepen your understanding of the financial markets and make you a better trader and investor.

16

About the Author

Malcolm Bucholtz, B.Sc, MBA is a graduate of Queen's University Faculty of Engineering in Canada and Heriot Watt University in Scotland where he received an MBA degree. After working in Canadian industry for far too many years, Malcolm followed his passion for the financial markets by becoming an Investment Advisor/Commodity Trading Advisor with an independent brokerage firm in western Canada. Today, he resides in western Canada where he trades the financial markets using technical chart analysis, esoteric mathematics and the astrological principles outlined in this book.

Malcolm is the author of several books. His first book, *The Bull, the Bear and the Planets*, offers the reader an introduction to Financial Astrology and makes the case that there are esoteric and astrological phenomena that influence the financial markets. His second book, *The Lost Science*, takes the reader on a deeper journey into planetary events and unique mathematical phenomena that influence financial markets. His third book, *De-Mystifying the McWhirter Theory of Stock Market Forecasting* seeks to simplify and illustrate the McWhirter methodology. Malcolm has been writing the Astrology Almanac each year since 2014.

Malcolm maintains both a website (www.investingsuccess.ca) and a blog where he provides traders and investors with astrological insights into the financial markets. He also offers a monthly **Astrology E-Alert** service where subscribers receive a bi-weekly previews of pending astrological events that stand to influence markets.

And, if all this were not enough, Malcolm now is pursuing studies towards an M.Sc. degree from Heriot Watt University in his other favorite area of pursuit Brewing & Distilling.

www.ingramcontent.com/pod-product-compliance
Lightning Source LLC
Chambersburg PA
CBHW071726200326
41519CB00021BC/6584